M000234050

GRACE SHIFT

By David Huskins

GRACE SHIFT

By David Huskins

BLAZE PUBLISHING
MANSFIELD, TEXAS

GRACE SHIFT
By David Huskins
Published by Blaze Publishing House
P.O. Box 184
Mansfield, TX 76063
www.blazepublishinghouse.com

This book or parts thereof may not be reproduced in part or in whole, in any form, stored in a retrieval system, or transmitted in any form by any means—electronic, mechanical, photocopy, recording, or otherwise—without prior written permission of the publisher, except as provided by United States of America copyright law.

Unless otherwise indicated, all Scripture quotations in this volume are taken from the *New King James Version* of the Bible, copyright © 1982 by Thomas Nelson, Inc. Used by permission. All rights reserved.

Scripture quotations marked NIV are taken from the *Holy Bible, New International Version*, copyright © 1973, 1978, 1984 by International Bible Society. Use by permission of Zondervan. All rights reserved.

Scripture quotations marked AMP are taken from the *Amplified Bible*. Old Testament copyright © 1965, 1987 by Zondervan Corporation, Grand Rapids, Michigan. New Testament copyright © 1958, 1987 by Lockman Foundation, La Habra, California.

Scripture quotations marked MSG are taken from *The Message*, copyright © 1993, 1994, 1995, 1996, 2000, 2001, 2002. Used by permission of NavPress Publishing Group.

Scripture quotations marked KJV are taken from the *Holy Bible, King James Version*.

Direct quotations from the Bible appear in italic type.

Cover design by Jay Hughes, Ingage Creative, jay@weingage.com. Photograph by istockphoto.com.

Manuscript Development by Kent Booth

Interior Design by Lisa Simpson
www.simpsonproductions.net

Copyright © 2010 by David Huskins

All rights reserved.

ISBN 10: 0-9792071-2-6

ISBN-13: 978-0-9792071-2-9

DEDICATION

I have this sense in my spirit that we are in the greatest transition in human history. It is certainly a shift from legalism to grace. However, it is also a transition from one generation to another. This generation—in whom I refer to as "Generation 42"—is poised and positioned to usher in a movement that will exceed the great reformation of Luther. It has the potential to operate in a power that will go beyond the outpouring of Azusa Street. This is the generation that will SHIFT from religion to Kingdom influence.

It is for this reason that I dedicate this writing to the generation that will come after me which includes not only my biological offspring, but also the sons and daughters of the Spirit that are preparing themselves now to stand in a ministry of no condemnation. It is the generation that will stand in power to show the glory of God to the ends of the earth. For you I breathe and write and live. You are the generation that will announce "IT IS FINISHED."

One such group of radical young leaders is the students who have captured my heart, passion, and spirit at Benson Idahosa University of Benin City, Nigeria. These Generation 42 men and women often have little in the natural to draw from but have chosen to give themselves to training to be the best for the Kingdom of God. They have the tenacity of the founder of their university—my dear friend and colleague the late Archbishop Benson Idahosa—the determination of their current chancellor and my covenant sister Archbishop Margaret Idahosa, and the fresh wisdom of the President of the University Dr. Feb Idahosa—my full covenant brother and spiritual son.

They will change the world.

Some years ago I became aware that many of the mentors and pioneers who have laid their hands on me for impartation were passing off the scene way too fast. My burden was that many coming after me would not know them or receive from them. I determined that must never be the case; therefore, I committed to making sure that wherever my voice was heard theirs would be also. When I lay hands on the next generation it will be through and by the impartation of the ones who laid hands on me. There must be no break of generational anointing.

I dedicate this book to each of the students of BIU and everyone of their generation who are determined not to operate under the Law but grace, and excel in mercy and not judgment. I pray that you will experience the shift from religion to relationship, and by the empowering force of Gods' grace, you would change your world.

I am also very honored by my natural sons, one of whom wrote the foreword to this book. I am also honored to be entrusted by God to leave a mark and legacy on this entire next generation. No mark I would rather leave than to share the liberating message of God's grace with each of you. What I have received I give to each of you.

I dedicate this book to the generation of Llaerton Michael, David Aaron, Zachary Caleb, and Jeremy Isaac. It is this generation that will change the world with the grace of God. I charge each of you to dream God's dream for the earth and by His grace re-dream it and redeem it.

Archbishop David Huskins

TABLE OF CONTENTS

FOREWORD

For too long, the church has placed its priority on judging people rather than showing them Christ. By disqualifying people and making them feel that they are not good enough, religion has run many away and caused them to completely write off church and even God. The worst part is what they have written off is not God; instead, it is an attitude that makes them feel unwanted. God is love—the love the hurting world so desperately needs. Sadly, on many occasions, the Church has failed to show that love.

I, for one, was a result of this same tragedy.

There was a time when I felt my life was over. Religion and the Church said that I was not good enough or did not have what it took to continue on. Only one thing saved my life—God's GRACE! I never had to beg or ask for His grace; I always had it simply because He loves me. God's mercy and acceptance lifted me back up to a real relationship with Him.

Many people believe that scaring "sinners" by threatening them with hell will make them want to live right. However, this theory faults by developing a fear of God without relationship. It is out of relationship that we learn who we really are in Christ. We make mistakes, and we learn from them. The difference is relation-ship. Out of fear, we regret momentarily, and for ourselves, we try to earn our way to Heaven. In relationship, we learn that certain things break God's heart, and out of our love for Him, we strive to please Him.

The real love of God shifts lifestyles, attitudes, and entire worlds. We do not have to force people to change who they are, for the love and grace of God reminds them of who they are: His righteous children. No matter how many times we fall, He will always keep forgiving, accepting, and loving us. Our God will never leave us nor forsake us.

Yes, it is possible that someone could take advantage of God's love, but why would anyone want to and misuse it? Many Christians are upset about this. They feel it gives people the right to do whatever they want without consequences. My question is, "What is it that these Christians feel they have been deprived of doing?" Once I experienced God's love, I understood that hell is not punishment for my sins. Hell is living a life without knowing the grace and love of God.

God's love and grace has been shown to me by Bishop David Huskins. I have known Bishop Huskins my entire life, and I consider myself blessed. He has shown me how to love the way God does, unconditionally and eternally, and also to accept people for who they truly are and not for what they have done, to love who they are and not judge or condemn them because of their current circumstances. I can testify that David Huskins is a man of grace and covenant who stands by those whom he is in relationship with, striving to show the same love and grace to everyone he knows.

He has also taught me, by example, the powerful love of a father. A father's love covers and protects. It always accepts and never fails. A true father always loves and always forgives. A true father never gives up on his son and will wait with open arms, no matter how long it takes. Without a true father, I never would have been able to believe in myself. Once revealed to the love of a father, one can truly comprehend the "SHIFT" that God's love and grace will have on his or her life.

I am blessed to know the love of a true father, and he has mentored and shown me how to love. I know a father's love because Bishop David Huskins—the man who introduced me to the love and grace of God—is my father. I am so blessed because my spiritual father is also my natural father.

This book is so vital for both the Believer and the non-believer because God's love is not exclusive to one or the other. God is love, period. There are no exceptions. I can think of no one better qualified to teach about God's grace than my dad. I love you, DAD. Thank you for showing me how to love like God. I am honored to be your son. The lessons I have learned just by watching you have honestly saved my life in ways you will never know.

David Aaron Huskins
Firstborn Son of Archbishop David Huskins

CHAPTER 1

NO, NOT ONE!

If you spend much time around Bible-believing Christians, you will quickly find out something: they love to quote the Word! Oh, yeah. It doesn't take long for someone to burst out The Beatitudes, The Lord's Prayer, or something from the Epistles. Even a simple prayer over a meal can turn into the Sermon on the Mount! Now, don't get me wrong; learning and meditating on the Word of God is a great discipline and a spiritual principle every Believer should adhere to. But if you're not careful, what you read can become dangerous and debilitating to you! That's right. Just reading and living in certain parts of the Bible—and not understanding the *whole counsel* of God—can keep you more bound than free . . . more mad than happy . . . more tied to legalism than grace!

Now, we're just in the second paragraph of the first chapter and already you might be thinking, "Oh, my Lord! This man just told me that reading the Bible was wrong!" No, that's not what I said at all. Allow me to explain. I LOVE the Bible. It's God's holy Word, given to us as a roadmap of how to live the Kingdom life. It contains over 6,000 promises that belong to each and every one of us. It truly is the lamp to our feet, the light to our path (Psalms 119:105), and the sustenance by which we live our lives. Jesus, Himself, said that man could never live on just mere bread, but on every Word that proceeds out of the mouth of God. (Matthew 4:4) The Bible itself is not the issue; the issue is . . .

. . . How some people read it!

Young people who are learning a musical skill or involved in little league sports always hear one word drilled into their heads: practice! They hear it a thousand times, "Practice, practice, practice. Do it over and over again." For years, whether it was sports, music, or drama, I would always tell my sons, "Boys, keep practicing, because practice makes perfect." Even though for an encouraging parent this sounds like the "right thing" to say, I've found out that statement really isn't true. The truth is: Perfect practice makes perfect! Think about it. If someone is trying to master a craft, play an instrument, or excel in a sport, and they keep practicing the wrong technique over and over again, guess what? They are never going to get any better. All they will do is perfect the wrong way of doing it. It's *perfect* practice that makes perfect performances.

The same principle is true with Christians who read . . . and read . . . and read the Bible, but camp in all the wrong places. Sure, they might know a ton of Scripture, but when they open their mouths, it's usually a dead giveaway of what they have been reading. For instance, when asked about their walk with the Lord, they might answer, "Well, I'm just an old sinner saved by grace." This statement is in the same category as "practice makes perfect." It sounds good. It sounds religious. It sounds like the right and "humble" thing to say, but it's not the truth! The Bible *never* says that about any Christian . . . actually, quite the opposite.

The reason so many God-loving Christians still have this type of mentality is because they have been religiously brainwashed instead of New Testament taught. It's much easier to hang onto old mindsets rather than to be renewed in their mind by the washing of the Word. (See Romans 12:2 and Ephesians 5:26.) Here is something else you will notice about this type of person. They always refer to Bible characters in their worst state of being. David is always a murderer, a liar, and an adulterer. Bartimaeus is always "blind Bartimaeus." Job is passionately referred to as "poor ole' Job." But none of these men stayed in these conditions! In the end, David is the only person God ever called "a man after My own heart." (Acts 13:22) Bartimaeus got healed! And Job received DOUBLE of everything he lost! (Job 42:10) Amazingly, all of these great endings are in the same Bible.

It's just a matter of how you read it.

A CHANGED VIEW

One very important thing I have come to know over the years is this: truth is a progression. As you walk with the Lord, God will continue to change the way you see Him. This is so important for the simple reason that the image of God you *believe* is the image of God you *become*. It also determines the way you show God to other people. If you think God is mean and hateful, guess what? You're probably going to be mean and hateful. If you think God doesn't like you, more than likely you will deal with acceptance issues your entire life. However, the more you get to know the real character and personality of God, the more of the *real* Him you project to others around you.

...the image of God you believe is the image of God you become.

When I was growing up as child, my image of God was a bit distorted mainly because of how those around me saw Him. Many times, I would hear statements like, "David, you better watch out. God is going to get you!" or "I don't know how much more God is going to take!" Of course, the one that really grabbed my attention was, "I think God has just about had enough of that!" I remember thinking, "Man, what happens when God finally *does* get fed up?" The answers I came up with just filled my heart with fear.

Those images even carried into my teenage years and early adulthood. I just knew that God was some angry, old man out there about 700 miles from Mars with a huge stick in His hand and His index finger resting on the "kill all" button! In my mind, all God was waiting on was for me, or someone around me, to step over the line—cross the point of no return—and then "zap." It would all be over but the dying and the crying.

What was happening to me? I was forming an image based on what those around me believed. What complicated it even more was all of the sermons I heard about how we were supposed to "love our enemies." I remember scratching my head thinking, "Now, wait a minute. We serve a God who is ready to kill us, His children, but we are supposed to love those who hate and despitefully use us? How can we do that?" To this day, this still makes no sense to me at all. But, thank God, I didn't stay in that state of mind.

A progression of truth started in my mind.

As I grew older and learned more about who God really was and not just what others said about Him, I began to see Him in a completely different light. The God I knew was a God of wrath, but the truth of His nature—His love and grace—was now being revealed in my heart. I began to see how the love of God drew people to Him and not the fear of going to hell or the dreaded "kill all" button. For the first time in my life, I was seeing God for who He really was.

While I loved this new perception *about* Him, I still lived far below my potential *in* Him. I was, once again, a product of what I heard. People were always quick to tell me how undeserving I was, how God required a holy life that I could never live, and no matter what I did, it would never be good enough to be considered "righteous." To make it even worse, they had Scripture to back up all of their theories and ideology. The only trouble was they were grossly misusing the Bible!

The truth is many Christians are still doing the same thing today.

DON'T STOP HALFWAY

Let's take for example one of the most misquoted verses in the New Testament. It's found in Romans chapter three. It's one of those scriptures many people learn early in their Christian walk, and sadly, wear it boldly like some holy badge of honor. The scripture I'm talking about is this:

"As it is written: 'There is none righteous, no, not one;'"

Romans 3:10

It's very obvious that this verse says no one is righteous. The problem is, most people stop right there. Religious-minded Believers will say, "See! Right there, the Bible says that not a one of us is righteous. We are all filthy rags and dogs in God's sight!" While this may sound good and "holy," the trouble is this passage doesn't stop there. It continues with an explanation of who this verse applies to, and guess what? It's not for the New Covenant Believer. Take a look:

"Now we know that whatever the law says, it says to those who are under the law . . ."

Romans 3:19

Seeing this verse in context, who does the Bible say is not righteous? It's easy to see: Those who are under the Law. This entire passage of Scripture—from verse 10 through verse 19—is actually a quote from the Old Testament that Paul uses to later prove a point. So, yes, while it is true the Old Testament Law says no one can live righteous, there is better news: *We have been redeemed from the curse of the law!* (Galatians 3:13) You see, it's not about what God is *going* to do; it's about what He has *already done* over 2000 years ago! The Church need not stop in any verse of the Bible which condemns us to unrighteousness, but move forward to understand that Jesus became our curse, took our unrighteousness, and paid the price for us to be and live in righteousness before God!

And the truth of that revelation is just beginning.

LEAVE THE OLD BEHIND

Remember, truth is progressive. You should always learn and grow in your revelation of truth. But, to move forward in God requires you to leave past things behind. Thank God, the blood of Jesus has covered your past sins, past failures, past mistakes, and past life; however, there is something else which lingers in the mind of most Christians which needs to be done away with as well. It's the old mindset of still living under the Old Testament Law.

Again, let me break some news to you that might be shocking: not everything in the Bible is for the New Testament Christian! A perfect example is the scripture seen in Romans, and there are many more examples. If you, as a New Covenant Believer, tried to apply every Old Testament Law to your life, you would be dead and in jail before you died. Under the Law, you could kill someone just because they didn't believe like you. Now, I wouldn't suggest using that part of the Old Covenant Law on someone you work with! You would probably find yourself starting a prison ministry—from the inside.

Most Christians would never think of doing something like that. Yet, on the other hand, they have no problem exercising the Law when they feel it's right or justified—especially to those they deem "deserve it." For example, some believe that a man who lives a perverted lifestyle should be killed. "That's what the Bible (or the Law) says to do." But, wait a minute. That same Law says anyone who

...not everything in the Bible is for the New Testament Christian!

plants two kinds of seed in the same field should be put to death as well. So, if you have both corn and beans in your backyard garden, too bad for you! The same Law says that any kind of manual labor on the Sabbath—even as much as turning on a light switch—is reason enough for the entire city to come out and stone you. Better watch your back on Sunday! And the list goes on and on. With so many rituals to keep, can you see why, under the Law, there was none righteous?

"No, not one!"

Many Christians have fallen into the trap where they dismiss the parts of the Law they don't agree with but still adopt the ones they like. They're quick to bang someone over the head with the Old Testament when it comes to things like tattoos, smoking, and drinking, saying, "If we don't like it, then God doesn't like it either." And God forbid if anyone is involved in the really "big sin" of homosexuality! Those are the ones God's really mad at, just like Sodom and Gomorrah. I've even heard Christians go so far to say that any homosexual who dies of AIDS, "Got what they deserved!" Really? Is this the rule the Church is going to play by? If so, then it has to apply to everyone—the "rank sinner" and the Church-going saint as well. We all need to "get what we deserve!"

> *We cannot judge others by their actions, while at the same time judge ourselves by our intentions.*

In reality, this is what's happening:

The Church justifies their actions by the Bible but validates their opinions by the Law!

The problem is you can't mix the two together. If we are going to enforce the Law on one, then it has to be the same for everyone. We cannot judge others by their actions, while at the same time judge ourselves by our intentions. We can't adhere to the portions of the Law that make us feel comfortable, but throw away the parts which address our own issues. If the adulterer is to be stoned, then we have to keep killing bulls to pay for our redemption. But, the truth is we don't have to live under the Law any longer! *Jesus came to fulfill all of the Law.* (Matthew 5:17) Not just some of it, part of it, or certain sections of it. He fulfilled it all and released us to live in something much stronger than the Law. It's called grace . . .

. . . God's amazing grace!

Still, even with knowledge of what Jesus provided on the cross, some Christians try to serve a New Covenant God while believing He behaves like an Old Covenant God. On one hand, they cry, "Grace, grace! God's grace," but still live under the fear that God is always mad at them, just waiting for them to step over the line, so He can push the button! They work and work and work, struggle and struggle and struggle just trying to do something "good enough" to earn God's forgiveness and grace. This type of Christian is usually easy to spot. They are frustrated, burned out, and live under so much self-condemnation that they never can enjoy being God's child.

Let me give you a spiritual principle that can change your life forever:

No one can ever be so good that they earn the grace of God, and no one can ever be so bad that they are disqualified from His grace!

One of the major characteristics about the Law is this: it is based on you. What *you* can and can't do, the things *you* did and didn't do, the manner in which *you* do things, even the days and times *you* can do it. But, thank God in Heaven, grace is not about what *you do*; it's completely and solely based on what *He did* and your ability to believe in it!

Contrary to what religious ideology wants you to believe, it really is that simple. Understand that religion has been—and always will be—connected and rooted in the Law. But real relationship with God, through His Son, Jesus, is 100% based on the grace God has provided. The only thing required of you now is to simply believe . . .

. . . Just like you did in the beginning.

WHAT BRINGS YOU, KEEPS YOU

If I were to ask you, "What did you do to get saved?" your answer would be pretty obvious. "Nothing! I just believed on Jesus and He saved me." That's exactly right. You did nothing except open up your heart and believe. Pretty simple, right? Well, now let me ask you another question. What do you think is required of you to *stay* saved and in relationship with God? The answer is exactly the same: just believe.

Many Christians fail to realize that whatever they did to get saved is what they will have to do to stay saved. Now, people who have been indoctrinated with religious thoughts can't seem to understand how simple this concept really is. They will argue, "Oh, no brother, we stay saved by how good we live and the good things we do." Well, that's not what we tell the sinner on the street, is it? Whenever someone comes forward in a church service for salvation, what's the first thing they hear? "Sir (or Ma'am) salvation is a free gift from God. All you have to do is BELIEVE and receive Jesus." If the first thing they heard was all the "stuff" required of them to become a Christian, they would probably turn and run out the back door!

You see, the gift of salvation starts out easy—by believing. But religion steps in and changes it from a gospel of *believing* to a gospel of *doing*! No longer is it about what we believe, but about what we do. This is not a modern-day Church problem; the Apostle Paul had to address the exact same issue with the church at Galatia. He wrote:

...whatever you did to get saved is what you will have to do to stay saved!

> **"You were running a good race. Who cut in on you to keep you from obeying the truth?"**
>
> **Galatians 5:7 (NIV)**

The Galatian Christians started out just like everyone else—by believing. But what happened? Religious teachers, who were still more connected to the Law than grace, stepped in and changed their course from believing to doing. The trouble is this exact same thing is still happening today. Maybe this has happened in your own Christian walk. Maybe you started off your journey like everyone else—by believing—but someone or something has cut in and kept you from obeying the truth. If so, let me give you a mind shift: *If believing brought you salvation, then only believing will keep you there!* The only issue is . . .

. . . What do you believe?

IT'S NOT HARD!

So many times over the years, I have heard people say something like, "Pastor David, I'm trying so hard to serve the Lord, but it is so difficult." Maybe you have even thought or said something to this effect in your Christian walk. If so, let me give you another statement that might make your brain tilt, but can really help relieve your frustrations:

> ***It's not hard to serve the Lord . . .***
> ***it's impossible!***

Before you think I've completely gone off the deep end, let me explain. There is only one person who can live this Christ-life— Christ. And guess what? You are not Him! But, that's okay. God knows you're not Christ. He knows you're not even close, even on your most holy, best-behaved, close-to-perfect day. You, I, or anyone else can't hold a candle to the perfection of our Messiah.

Now, if we lived under the Old Covenant Law, this would be very, very bad news. Under that regime, we could try and try and try to be righteous; but at the end of the day, none of us would be—"no not one." But remember, Christ redeemed us from the Law. Look at how Paul describes what happened the day Jesus died on the cross:

"For what the law could not do in that it was weak through the flesh, God did by sending His own Son in the likeness of sinful flesh, on account of sin: He condemned sin in the flesh,"

Romans 8:3

The Law was weak in the fact that it could never save us. Rules could never draw us close to God. Regulations could never make us anymore righteous than we were without Christ. The Law only connects you to sin and the weakness of your flesh. But, God canceled the Law and fulfilled every jot and tittle through Jesus. Why? So that we might be made "the righteousness of God through Christ." (2 Corinthians 5:21) Oh, thank God that Jesus took our sin, became our unrighteousness, and paved the way for us to live in right-standing before God.

It's our new life of grace!

THE LIFE OF GRACE

Over the next several pages, we are going to embark on a remarkable journey together—a journey out of the Law and into the truth of God's grace. As we begin, there is one thing I would like to address which, if not dealt with properly, can become very debilitating in your walk. It's the old idea that God is always mad at you! Nothing could be farther from the truth. Of course, the religious crowd will always remind you of how God poured out His wrath in the Old Testament; but again, it was the *Old Testament* ruled under the Law. Today, there is good news:

God took out all of his wrath on Jesus at the cross,
so you could fully live in His grace!

Now, through the shed blood of Jesus, the Bible says you can come boldly to the "throne of grace." (Hebrews 4:16) Notice, it's not the throne of wrath or judgment. When you come into God's awesome presence, here is one way the Bible says you should look:

"I will therefore that men pray every where, lifting up holy hands, without wrath and doubting."

1 Timothy 2:8 (KJV)

Why does the Bible say "holy hands?" Because that's the way God sees you—holy! You lift one hand without wrath: God's not angry with you, so you don't have to be angry any longer. You lift the other hand without doubt which says, "God's not mad at me, and there's absolutely no doubt about it!" No longer are you going to live in fear of His wrath but motivated by His grace.

> *"God's not mad at me, and there's absolutely no doubt about it!"*

The grace of God is, in fact, so amazing. The more truth that is revealed to you about His grace, the more you will fall in love with Jesus. He's the One who died and rose from the grave to pay your entire penalty and provide full access to God. Now's it time to leave behind the old Law and run into your new life of God's unmerited, unearned grace! Are you ready to make some changes? Is it time to adjust your thought pattern to align with God's Word? Better yet, are you ready for a shift that can change the entire way you live? If you are, then let's go!

It's time for a grace shift!

Chapter 2

The Realities of Righteousness

Have you ever stopped to notice just how reality driven our society has become? Everywhere you turn, people are star-struck by reality. Back in the 1970's, Coca-Cola® began an advertising campaign which said, "It's the real thing. Coke!" That slogan started a thirst (no pun intended!) for things that were really real. Some years later, world heavy-weight boxing champion Evander Holyfield termed himself "Evander the Real Deal Holyfield" and people went crazy over it. About that same time, many music and rap artists began releasing music with heavy, explicit lyrical content. After receiving much criticism from parents as well as the U.S. Congress, the record labels justified the use of such language as: "We're just keeping it real!" And their records sold by the millions. Why?

Because everyone loves reality.

The crave for reality has continued to increase over the years. Now, you can't turn on your television set, whether it's day or night, without coming across something called Reality Television. People watch it by the droves, and honestly, some of it is not even good programming! Today, ex-professional wrestlers, aged rock-and-roll musicians, and even families with a load of kids film their everyday lives and put it up for the world to see. And we watch it . . . by the millions. Every time famed American Idol host Ryan Seacrest announces, "And the person leaving the show tonight is . . .," people intently stare into the television screen, hold their breath, and gasp when the results are announced! Why?

Because we love reality!

While the world yearns for reality, the church world is a bit different. On the outside, we say all the right things that show our desire for revelation. We pray things like, "God, show us Your ways and Your truth," and we sing songs like, "Open my ears, so I can hear you. Open my heart so I can know You." All of these cries for the reality of God's Word sound great, but here's the problem: God begins to reveal His truth, but if it doesn't fit within our religious mindsets, then it's labeled as heresy and completely thrown out! In short, the Church says it wants the "real deal," but in reality, most of the time, they only want God to validate their religious thinking.

One of the subjects which falls into this category is the issue of Biblical, New Testament righteousness. Denominational wars have been fought and battles lost over what righteousness really means, how it's obtained, and how it impacts our lives as Believers. After all of the discussions and debates, most people's doctrine is still more laden with religious pretense than Biblical truth. The most frustrating part is, while we are telling people they should live "righteous," most people still have no idea what it even entails. For me, I think Christians are long overdue on knowing the truth about what God says concerning righteousness.

It's time Believers knew "the real deal."

If you're ready, then let's look at what the Bible says about this wonderful gift provided to us through God's amazing grace.

REALITY # 1
RIGHTEOUSNESS ONLY COMES FROM ONE SOURCE

We've already seen how grace and the Law contradict each other. The Law says you have to do something, while grace only requires you to believe something. The Law still has God mad at you, while grace activates God's love and mercy toward you. The Law says approaching God is like a child being sent to the principal's office while grace says, "Come unto me all who are weary." (Matthew 11:28) Since the majority of the Church is still Law-minded, it will take a double, triple, even quadruple dose of truth to change the way we have been taught.

In the book of Romans, chapter three, the Apostle Paul lays out one of the most beautiful exposés on the subject of righteousness. Now, when most Christians hear anything about this chapter, they immediately go to verse 23: "For all have sinned and come short of the glory of God." Believe me, we have that scripture down pat and are quick to tell anyone how lost, sorry, and sinful they are!

But, let's jump up a few verses and see how Paul really sets up this entire passage.

The first 20 verses of Romans chapter three clearly describe how none of us are righteous by the Law. Many times, we quote those verses as if they were New Testament doctrine when in actuality most of those 20 verses are quotes from the Old Testament. When you look at the entire context of the chapter, you can see where Paul is only laying a foundation, from the Law, to then reveal how the New Covenant differs. Verse 21 is the first New Covenant principle in this chapter that says:

> *"But now the righteousness of God apart from the law is revealed, being witnessed by the Law and the Prophets,"*
>
> **Romans 3:21**

If you're not careful, you will blow right past the two most important words in this entire scripture: the first two words— *"but now."* Let me quickly explain how these two words are used. Anytime in the Bible you see these two words together, it means that whatever preceded them doesn't apply to what is about to be said. For example, in Ephesians 2:11-12, Paul describes our state of being before we came into the saving knowledge of Christ. According to these scriptures, we were lost and alienated from God without hope. Then verse 13 has a shift in focus as it begins with, *"But now* in Christ . . ."* For the next several verses, Paul emphasis changes from where we were before Christ to our new life in Christ all following "But now."

This is precisely the same principle found here in Romans chapter three. What Paul is saying at the beginning of verse 21 is

"Everything that has preceded is not connected to what is about to follow." In other words, "Is there any righteous? No, not one. But now . . .!" Now that you understand this structure a bit more clearly, take another look at that same verse. What you see just might be a life-changing revelation.

> **"But now the righteousness of God apart from the law is revealed, being witnessed by the Law and the Prophets,"**

After laying out 20 verses of what the Law has to say about you, Paul's first "But now" statement is powerful: Righteousness that comes from God has absolutely nothing to do with the Law. Just knowing that fact alone can set you free! Not only does Paul know this to be true, but to validate his point even further, he has witnesses to back it up: the Law itself and the Prophets of the Old Covenant. Now, isn't it funny how the Old Testament Prophets—men who lived thou sands of years before you and me—said, "Yes, this is right! We agree! The Law we live under can

Righteousness that comes from God has absolutely nothing to do with the Law.

never produce a righteous state. Righteousness is from God alone." And, here's something else that's amazing: *They received this revelation centuries before Jesus came to the Earth!* Yet, Christians today, with Bible in hand, struggle with this simple truth!

Just like the entire message of grace is simple and easy, so is righteousness reality number one. When Jesus died on the cross, not only did He redeem our lives from hell, he also became sin for us so we could be the righteousness of God!

REALITY #2
RIGHTEOUSNESS ONLY COMES ONE WAY

This reality of righteousness, even though once again simple, is probably one of the most difficult to activate and live. Honestly, I believe a second-grade child could read the beginning of this next verse and have an understanding of what it says. But, again, the religious can't keep the Bible simple! They want to make it more complicated than it really is. So, I challenge you to take off those religious-shaded glasses and take a fresh look at verse 22.

"Even the righteousness of God, through faith of Jesus Christ . . ."

Romans 3:22

Do you see what it says? It's pretty plain English, isn't it? After Paul establishes that the Law is no longer the way to right-standing with God, he very clearly relays how you can obtain it—*by faith in Jesus Christ!* Notice, there is not a multiple choice list of how you become righteous. There's no martyrdom required or no long, drawn-out process of rites and passages. There are no rituals and ceremonies—none of these things. As simple as it may seem, you become righteous in God's sight by one way:

HAVING FAITH IN THE LORD
JESUS CHRIST

Here's a mind shift for you: Being a "good Christian" or a "good person" can never produce a righteous state of being! Never. Righteousness is a *position*, not based on a *performance*, and only comes as a free gift from God to those who believe. So, the person who's been "good" all of his or her life is no more righteous, based solely on their works, than the person who has lived a "bad" life. So many "good" people try to earn their righteousness and even have a litany of qualifications which should, at least in their mind, guarantee their right-standing with God. They say, "Now, God, you know all the good things I do. I fast. I pray. I give. I feed the hungry. I even work in the nursery, and you know how much I don't like little snotty-nosed kids. I don't smoke, drink, run around on my mate . . .," and the list continues. Even though these are good things, here's the problem:

> *Righteousness is a position, not based on a performance*

They all revolve around the word "I."

The truth is that no matter how much "I" does, it can never equate to what "He" has already done! When Christians finally realize this truth—that all of their good works never made them any more righteous than the sinner on the street—they usually get mad! They're not necessarily mad at God, but mad at themselves. Why? Because they have done all this work . . . all for naught! It reminds me of when my sons started to realize Santa Claus was not real. Whether they were "naughty or nice" really didn't make any difference. There would have still been presents under the tree on Christmas Day.

The spiritual principle that righteousness comes only by believing actually started in the Old Covenant, under the Law. Do you remember the only person who was called "righteous" by God in the Old Testament? It wasn't David, Noah, Joseph, Daniel, Jeremiah, or even Moses. It was Abraham, also known as the "father of faith." And how was Abraham counted as righteous? The Bible clearly explains:

> *"And the Scripture was fulfilled which says, 'Abraham believed God, and it was accounted to him for righteousness.'"*
>
> **James 2:23**

Even though Abraham did many wonderful things to obey God, including committing to offer up his Son, Isaac, as a sacrifice, none of the things he did counted to him as righteous. Only one thing moved him into that place—*he believed God!*

Now, your mind might be telling you, "Oh, that was easy for Abraham; he was the father of faith. It can't be that easy for me." But, that's the whole point—IT IS THAT EASY! Tyrannical preachers want you to believe righteousness is connected to what you do and something only the "good Christians" obtain, but that's not what the Bible says! This scripture clearly reemphasizes this point: To be righteous, the Law said you must *do*, but grace says you must *only believe!*

REALITY #3
RIGHTEOUSNESS IS FOR EVERYONE

Once some people see the Scriptures for what they really say, they can digest the fact that God is the source of righteousness; mainly because, it's connected with Jesus' death on the cross. Then, there is the group (not as vast as the first) who grab the simplicity of just believing. But, this next step—the reality that righteousness is not exclusive to a certain set group of people—is where many Christians jump off the boat! One thing I have found to be true is that the more religion someone has been taught, the harder it is to connect with this Biblical truth. Again, look how Paul describes it:

> *"Even the righteousness of God which is by faith of Jesus Christ unto all and upon all them that believe . . ."*
>
> **Romans 3:22 (KJV)**

Notice two very key phrases: "unto all," and "upon all." Even though they sound similar, they both carry very different connotations. When you see them in their context, they begin to paint the picture of God's amazing grace to all Mankind.

- **Unto all.** First, Paul specifically declares that righteousness from God, received through faith in Jesus, has no restrictions, limitations, or boundaries. What this means is that in God's eyes, the mass murderer is just as righteous as the saint who has been in church for the last 50 years and has never as much broken the speed limit. The person who comes into the Kingdom at the eleventh hour is just as righteous as those who have worked all their life for the same blessing. Thank God this scripture doesn't give qualifications such as, "This is only for those who have worked, labored, and toiled for it," or, "It's only for those who are good enough," because if it did, *you or I would not even come close to qualifying!*

When Jesus died, He paved the way for all humanity to have full access to God. He was truly saying, "Come one, come all. No matter what you are or what you've done, now you have direct access to my Father!" Righteousness is available to everybody.

- **Upon all.** While righteousness is for everybody, not everybody walks in righteousness. Why? Because God's righteousness is only given to those who believe it. So many Christians live far below their privileges simply because their religious mind just won't let them believe they are what the Bible says they are: "The righteousness of God through Christ!" While God's amazing promise and gift is right before them and all around them, they chose to walk away and not receive what has already been provided through Jesus' ultimate sacrifice on the cross.

> *While righteousness is for everybody, not everybody walks in righteousness!*

Imagine the person who wants a new car for Christmas. (Maybe that's you!) Christmas Day comes, and there sets their brand new car parked in the driveway. Someone hands them the keys and all they have to do is get in and drive. How tragic would it be for this same person to walk around that car, feel the outside body, sit in the comfy leather seats—even crank up the CD player—but never take it for a ride? What if they just gave the keys back and said, "Oh, this is too good to be true! I just can't believe this is mine!"? The thing they desired is right in front of them, but if they never believe it actually belongs to them, they will never enjoy the pleasure and benefits it can provide.

It is the same way with righteousness. Jesus paid the price in full for everyone to live in right-standing with God. The only issue is who is going to believe it? Who will be the one who stands up in the midst of the religious crowd and boldly proclaims, "Hey, I'm a Believer! This is for me, right now!"? If it's you, then you will be the one whose righteousness is not only "unto" but "upon."

In my mind, I think everyone who hears this awesome truth would just jump up and shout, "Yes, Lord! Thank You for providing the way for *everyone* to be counted as righteous!" Not so. Even though they may love the fact that *they* are righteous, the last part of this verse—four little words—can generate an entirely different response. As a matter of fact, I probably have read this passage in Romans hundreds of times before I ever realized these four powerful words ever existed. But when I saw them, God began to radically change the way I thought. Look at how the Apostle Paul ends this great passage:

"For there is no difference!"

Romans 3:22b

Isn't it amazing how we can just read right over something for years and then, one day, God just stops us in our tracks and says, "Hey, pay attention to this!"? That's exactly what happened to me one day when these words flew off the page. Immediately, I began to weep, repent, and then asked the Lord, "God why doesn't the Church treat people like this? Why don't we see people like you see them—through the shed blood of Your Son, Jesus? Why do we have to categorize people?" Then, the answer became clear in my heart. Our reluctance to the acceptance of this truth is rooted in our competitive nature.

Yes, even as Christians!

Don't get me wrong, most Believers have enough compassion to rejoice with the outcast who finds Jesus. But, what they can't handle is the fact that this brand new Believer is, in the eyes of God, immediately just as righteous as they are! What drives the older Christian crazy is realizing they have worked all these years to earn their righteousness . . . *and they didn't have to.* Some even protest by saying something like, "God, that's just not fair. What I've had to do, they should be required to do as well." Well, there's only one problem with that statement: The righteousness of God has nothing to do with Him being "fair." Actually, the Bible never says that God is "fair," but that He is "just" which means this wonderful gift of righteousness is available for all and unto all who will simply believe it.

In God's eyes, there truly is "no difference." Hallelujah, we all qualify!

REALITY #4
RIGHTEOUSNESS IS GOD'S GRACE IN ACTION

Immediately following God's amazing provision of righteousness is one of the most familiar verses in the Bible—Romans 3:23. This is a great verse, but for years we have put more emphasis on the sinful nature of Man, and it's amazing how young we are when this indoctrination begins.

Many years ago, a grade-school child who was enrolled in a Christian school came up to me and said, "Pastor David, I am learning my ABC's by using Bible verses." I thought to myself, "Man, what a great idea. Learning the ABC's by using the Bible." When it was all said and done, this boy would have memorized 26 verses of the Bible. What a great concept! Then I asked him, "Son, what is the first verse you learn for the letter A?" He said, "Oh that was easy. We learned 'A—All have sinned and come short of the glory of God!'" I immediately thought, "What? Why that verse? Why not 'A merry heart does good like a medicine,' or 'Ask and you shall receive'?" It was a great concept, but in my mind, the wrong application. Not to mention that the verse they used doesn't even start with the letter A! It begins with the letter F—"For all have sinned . . ." Can you see how, even at a young age, we are so quick to accentuate our fallen, sinful nature?

And even use the Bible to back it up.

The truth is, Romans 3:23 is more about God's incredible grace than it is our sinful nature. But, like we saw in our last chapter, it's how you read it. Take a look at this scripture one more time:

"For all have sinned, and come short of the glory of God;"

Romans 3:23 (KJV)

Look at this word: have. All *have*, (have, past tense, in the past) *have* sinned and missed the fullness of God. What does this mean? It means that God's grace has already paid the price for the remission of your sins . . . long before you even committed one! If you're a Christian, then you believe Jesus died on the cross for your sins, right? But, wait a minute. When Jesus died for your sins, you weren't even born yet, still Jesus was washing and redeeming your sins long before your physical existence on this planet. The awesomeness of this truth is this: Your sins were *past* before they were even *present!* Now, your brain might really be tilting, but look how the following verses describe how this happened:

"Being justified freely by His grace through the redemption that is in Christ Jesus, whom God set forth as a propitiation by His blood, through faith, to demonstrate His righteousness, because in His forbearance God had passed over the sins that were previously committed,"

Romans 3:24-25

How are you justified? By God's wonderful grace through redemption in Christ. The sins Jesus redeemed you from are the ones in the past through the forbearance of God. Put in simpler terms, God saw your sins, put up with them, forbore them, and removed your sins before you had even breathed your first breath of air in this life! Friend, this is God's grace in action. Redemption is not what you did, but rather you believe what God did. And, *if you can believe it*, here is another bit of good news:

YOU ARE RIGHTEOUS . . . just as Jesus was righteous!

It's God's unexplainable grace in action.

NEVER BE ASHAMED

The only way you, I, or any other person is justified is through the Justifier—Jesus Christ. Years ago, I heard a preacher of true righteousness say it this way, "When I believed Jesus justified my sin, it's just-as-if-I-had never sinned to begin with!" This was not only a great play on words and a catchy phrase; it was the eternal truth of this scripture. Jesus is our justification. When the devil comes to bring condemnation on you for something you did years ago, just remind him who your validation comes from! It's the exact same person that defeated him (the devil) and took away his right to condemn any child of God—including you!

The book of Revelation clearly says that we all will face accusations from our enemy. Things like, "You're no good. How can you stand up and say you're righteous when you know what you've done," and more. But, it also gives the spiritual key to how we overcome these false allegations. The Bible says we have victory by two ways:

"And they overcame him by the blood of the Lamb and by the word of their testimony,"

Revelation 12:11

Thank God Jesus shed His spotless blood to cover our sins, but He also gave us the right to speak, or to testify, how He has made us the righteousness of God! And what is our testimony? "The Justifier has made us just!" So, the next time someone says, "You should be ashamed of yourself," you should rear your head up and say, "No, He took my shame! Jesus bore my guilt, so I don't have to!" You're not admitting that you are proud of everything you have done in your past, but rather proclaiming that God has covered you and is still working on you.

There are no second-class citizens in the Kingdom of God. No one takes a second seat to anyone, but we don't a take a seat in front of anyone as well. We all sit in the same seat—the seat of righteousness which was made possible and sealed through God's remarkable grace. Now, it's left up to you. It's time to walk in the righteousness Jesus purchased for you on the cross. Time to know the "real deal" and live the real, righteous life God has enabled you to live. Start to shift your thoughts and let the *real* image of God become alive in your heart, enabling you to share the good news of His grace to those around you. When you do, watch out. Things are about to change.

The shift is on!

CHAPTER 3

REAL CHANGE

The day you believed and said, "Yes," to Jesus, something happened. You changed! Now you probably looked exactly the same on the outside, but something drastically changed in your inner-man. At that very moment, your spirit-man moved from death to life, from darkness to light, and you left a state of being lost to becoming a child of the living God! This transformation is so radical that Jesus termed it as being "born again." (John 3:3) Literally, in a split second, your old man died and the new you came alive in Christ Jesus.

The new birth transformation is something most every Christian—even the ultra-religious crowd—can agree on. We all shout, "Hallelujah, another sinner was saved by grace," but after their initial conversion, so many people are quick to abandon the grace which led them to salvation in the first place. Instead of walking in grace and growing in grace, they automatically go back to what they have always known—the works of the flesh. But, whose fault is it that these new Christians leave God's grace? Can new babies in Christ really be held completely responsible to walk this new experience by themselves? I don't think the issue lies with the new Believer, but more with those who indoctrinate them with religious, Law-based, traditional thinking.

Think of a natural baby. What would happen if two weeks after he/she was born, their parents said, "Ok, you're alive in this world now, our job is over. Learn the best way you can!"? I'll tell you what would happen. Those parents would end up in jail with the key thrown far away! Yet, over and over again, spiritual babies are left to figure out how to walk with God all by themselves. Or, even worse, someone who is still entangled with the Law immediately begins to pollute their mind with what they *think* is the New Testament way to live. Soon, what started as "Oh, brother, just *believe*," changes to "Now, brother, this is what you have to *do* . . ."

But, *believing* and *doing* almost always contradict each other!

Is it any wonder why so many Christians—even those who have been saved for a number of years—are still spiritual babies? They still have to drink spiritually predigested, processed milk, still have to be spoon-fed every meal, and some can't even walk on their own. Think about a natural child who is in the fifth grade, but still brings a bottle of baby formula to school every day for lunch. You would probably say, "That child's parents need to be whipped." and rightfully so. But, in the Church, we just let people crawl around in spiritual diapers for years without holding their spiritual teachers accountable.

I believe it's time to speak what the Bible says and break the chains of religion, so Christians can be set free. I can't think of any place better to start than to look at how God's Word says change—real, authentic, long-lasting change—takes place in the life of a Believer.

BACK TO THE BEGINNING

Go back to the day you were born again. Did you have to work up anything? No. You came to Jesus a mess, and in one instant, you left changed. You were only required to do one thing: believe. Stone cold drunks can come to Jesus so intoxicated that they can't even spell their name, and in one moment, be changed for eternity. Most of the time, they can't even tell you what happened, but one thing they do know: God, by His grace, reached down and transformed their entire life. Not just for the drunkards, but for anyone who is a Believer, the salvation process was a breeze . . . but what follows the new birth experience is where people really struggle.

All of my life I have watched good-hearted, God-loving Christians battle with inner-personal issues until the day they went to Heaven. They weren't bad people or backsliders, most of the time, just the opposite. They loved God and were committed to follow Him all the days of their life but they were constantly battling the same things over and over again. Honestly, I never could quite understand why such good people could always be tormented . . . and defeated . . . by the same one or two issues and never experience real, long-lasting change and victory. Then one day, while studying about God's grace, the answer hit me.

And, it wasn't even that hard to see!

If you were to ask these people about a certain area of temptation or weakness of their flesh, they normally would say, "Oh, keep praying for me brother. I'm working on overcoming it!" This might have been the "right" and religious thing to say, but in reality, it pinpointed the foundation of their problem. The reason they kept having the same battles (and losing the same battles!) was because *they* were *working* on it! It was all about them—what *they* were *doing* in their own power and strength to overcome the issues. It sounded good, but here is the fallacy of that mindset: The first day they didn't work at it, they were right back in it!

Maybe you have caught yourself saying this same thing or something similar. You might even be one of those "holy ones" who uses the Scripture to back your self-waged war by saying, "I'm working out my salvation just like the Bible says to." Well, true, you might be working on something alright, but in reality, that weakness and temptation is probably *working on you* more than you are *working on it!* One day, you have the victory, and the next day you're back doing what you promised God you would never do again. Let me assure you of one thing: This cycle of frustration will never go away until one thing happens . . .

. . . You experience real change!

THE MIXED BAG

Practically every Christian I know has lived, at one time or another, what I call the "mixed bag" of Christianity. They seem to constantly vacillate between blessing and cursing. One day they have a breakthrough, and the next day it's hell on earth! It's victory one week, and "Pray for me, the devil's on my back" the next week. Now, don't get me wrong, as long as you and I breathe air there will always be temptations and battles. But when we understand and embrace the power of real change through God's grace, we start living—like the Bible says—from "faith to faith" and from grace to grace! (Romans 1:17)

So, what brings the real change we all strive for in our lives? Well, let me start by giving you another mental shift. It is this:

Real change requires no effort!

I can already see you scratching your head and thinking, "What? I can really change without doing one thing?" The answer is, "Yes, you can!" I know because for years I tried to do everything just right (remember I thought God had his finger on the "zap all" button!), and all it produced was a life of frustration, condemnation, and broken promises to God. No matter how many times I said, "God, I will never do that again," I would still end up doing "that" again. Of course, I could always justify my weakness by quoting the words of Jesus: "The spirit is indeed willing but the flesh is weak." (Matthew 26:41) What I forgot to realize was what Jesus was addressing in that passage—the strength to pray, not the weakness of His flesh!

The will to pray wasn't my issue at all. I could pray all day, every day, but still lived the "mixed bag" Christian life. As a matter of fact, I thought praying more would give me the strength to overcome my flesh. So, I ramped up my prayer time. Guess what? It didn't help me change one thing. Then I figured that if more prayer wasn't going to help me defeat these hounding issues, surely fasting would be the key. So, I fasted. And guess what happened? I lost weight (which wasn't a bad thing!), but was cranky to everyone around me, and I constantly griped about how hungry I was!

Still, no change.

After many years of frustration and self-condemnation, without much lasting results, I knew there had to be another way. I also knew countless others Christians who were being held under this same, demonic mindset. And they, just like I, yearned to be free. So, I began my quest to find real answers, real truth, and real change. This journey was actually two-fold: To rid myself of wrong, religious indoctrination that had permeated my mind, and to find out exactly what God's Word had to say about real change.

What I discovered completely changed my life!

STEPS TO REAL CHANGE

Instead of finding a bunch of scriptures that dealt with "change," I found more and more truth in the Bible about what causes life-long change: *God's amazing grace!* The more I studied, the clearer this incredible message of grace began to live inside my heart. And, today, it's still growing, developing, and becoming the message that is setting me and many other people free—free to actually be and live what God has called us all to be.

So, what about you? Are you ready to leave that old "mixed bag" Christian life of frustration and guilt? If so, here are some steps that I believe will help you leave the old way behind, experience real-life change, and fall more in love with the grace of God. These are more than just good theories and concepts. I know they work! Open your heart and get ready . . .

. . . Ready to experience real change!

#1

CHANGE YOUR BELIEF SYSTEM

To initiate real, long-lasting change, first and foremost you must revolutionize your belief system. What this means is that you transform the way you believe, or have been taught, and start aligning your thoughts with God's Word. Before you start to think, "Oh, well that's easy," let me give you a dose of reality. Changing your belief system takes work—and a lot of it! Depending on how much you have been incorrectly taught will determine how much readjusting will be required. The good news is it *can* be done, and when you begin to see how God *really* sees you, it will release you to become the follower of Jesus He has made you to be!

One of the most important ways to have a shift in your belief system is by changing what you hear. The Bible clearly says that faith comes by hearing, and hearing, and hearing, and hearing. (Romans 10:17) Well, faith isn't the only thing that grows by hearing. Doubt, condemnation, unbelief, and religious thinking all come the same way: by hearing! It's simple. If you are

Changing your belief system takes work—and a lot of it!

constantly surrounded by those who keep reminding you what a "bad person" you used to be (or maybe still are), then you need to change your surroundings. Get around people who will tell you what God really says you are: righteous, holy, and redeemed! It's the first step in changing the way you believe.

A few years ago, I started inserting a statement right in the middle of my messages that I knew would catch people's attention. I used it to prove a powerful point; but honestly, I think it's just as much fun to watch people's reaction! After giving a scripture reference to the audience, I say, "Now, I want everybody in this room who is holy to read this verse out loud with me." Then, I just stand there and watch! The different responses are priceless. They range from "What did he just say?" to "Holy? Well, he sure isn't talking about me!" (Sometimes I think I would get a better response if I cursed in the middle of my message!) Just when everyone has that cow-at-a-new-gate look, I take it a bit further and say, "Hey, if you're a Believer, *you're the one I'm talking to!*"

We need a belief system makeover!

Now, if I were to say, "I want every person who used to be an old sinner to open and read with me," practically everybody in the place would say, "Amen, brother. That's me!" Do you see where we've missed it? Why is it so easy to relate and connect to what we *used* to be, but so hard to identify with we *now are* by God's grace? The answer is simple: We need a belief system makeover! We need to start believing what the Bible—not religious doctrine—says about us.

Remember, what you believe, you become. Thus, if you are going to live and experience real change, you must first change the way you believe to align your thoughts with what God says about you!

#2

SEE HIM LIKE HE IS

Have you ever heard people say things like, "I can't wait to get to Heaven because then I'm going to see Jesus for who he really is."? Even though there is some merit to this statement—one day we will see Jesus face-to-face—not examining what the Scripture says can cause you to miss something God really intended for you here, right now, on this earth.

Take a look at what the Bible says:

> *"Beloved, now we are children of God; and it has not yet been revealed what we shall be, but we know that when He is revealed, we shall be like Him, for we shall see Him as He is."*

1 John 3:2

It would be easy to see how you could read this verse and only relate it to God revealing Himself in Heaven. But, that's not where the power of this scripture is found. You see, God's not waiting for you to get to Heaven to disclose His power and nature to you. He wants to reveal Himself to you *right now* . . . through His Word! You don't have to wait until the Second Coming to have a revelation of Him; you can find Him, today, in the Scripture. This is so important to understand for this one, simple fact:

Whatever Him you see is the Him you'll be!

Go back and see how this verse starts out. It says, "Beloved, now we are children of God . . ." Most Christians completely skip over the most important word of this verse—"*now*." When? Now! Then the question is, "When is 'now'?" and the answer is, "Right now!" Not in the sweet bye-and-bye; not someday, sometime, in some place. It's not one day in the future when you've done enough good things and deserved to be called a child of God. NO. Look at what the Bible says, "*Now*, we are the children of God." That means the second you believed, right that instant, you qualified for this verse. There's no waiting period.

NOW you are a child of God!

And guess what children do? In most cases, they strive to mimic their parents! Why do you think little boys cover their soft, young faces with shaving cream and little girls prance around in high heels way too big for them and color their faces with make up? It's because children's inherent nature is to be like their parents. And when they do the little things to become like mom or dad (even at a young age), it makes those parents blossom with pride! It's the same way spiritually. The Bible says that we should be "imitators of God as dear children." (Ephesians 5:1) Every child of God should be imitating their Heavenly Father. But, instead of learning the real nature and char-acteristics of their Heavenly Father, most Christians spend the

The more of Him that's revealed in you the less you see of you!

majority of their time on another issue: battling their own weaknesses and failures.

Everyone knows their own weaknesses and areas of struggle in the flesh; they greet you every morning as soon as you look into the mirror! But, have you ever stopped to think why these areas of weaknesses in your life are so prevalent and easy to see? It's simple. They have been revealed to you over and over again. As a matter of fact, some Christians are reminded about them every single Sunday—in church nonetheless—from a preacher who wants to keep them more bound to their weakness than free in God's grace.

And we wonder why so many Believers stay in a spiritual rut!

Long-lasting, real change starts to develop once you change your belief system and start seeing God for who He really is. Stop concentrating on the areas where you are weak. (Believe me, they will always be there!) Begin to focus and learn who God is. Allow Him to reveal Himself to you through His Word. When you do, something amazing will happen: The more of Him that's revealed in you the less you see of you!

This is how real change happens.

#3
YOU MUST SAY "YES!"

During the 1980's and early 1990's, a campaign was launched which was part of the United States' war on drugs. Millions of dollars

...before you can just say, "No" to something, you must first say, "Yes" to something greater!

were spent to make sure every child in America knew these three, famous words: Just Say No. It's original intent was to discourage children from engaging in recreational drug use, but after a few years, the scope broaden to include the realms of violence, pre-marital sex, and other issues in which young people were tempted to participate.

The "Just Say No" slogan was a good catch phrase and produced some positive, mostly short-term results; however, it was lacking one very important element which produces long-term change. You see, before you can just say, "No" to something, you must first say, "Yes" to something greater! Just saying, "No" to temptation and the weaknesses of your flesh is not enough. Many people say, "No," but turn right around and do the same thing over and over again. And what happens when this method doesn't work? It produces more frustration than victory—more condemnation than change.

As if the guilt of making the same mistakes over and over again isn't enough to carry, some Christians heap more blame on their heads by asking, "Why am I resisting the devil, just like the Bible says, but he's not going away?" They try and try to say, "No" to every attack of the enemy, yet with little results. Well, the answer to their frustration is found in the exact same verse they referred to. Take a look at this verse in its entirety:

"Therefore submit to God. Resist the devil and he will flee from you."

James 4:7

Here's the missing ingredient: Resisting the devil (a.k.a. just saying no) is only half of the equation. In order to live a life of constant victory over your flesh, something else has to happen first. You must submit to God. You cannot have the power to say, "No" to sin without first saying, "Yes" to the only sustaining force that can keep you from sin. In other words, *without a submission to righteousness, it is impossible to resist sin.* Trying to fight the devil and conquer your flesh in your own strength will not only keep you in the vicious cycle of defeat, it will also drive you crazy! But, there is a way to stand against the devil and watch him run from you: by completely submitting your life to the powerful grace of God.

If submitting to God is the key to victory over the devil, then why do so many Christians still struggle with temptation and sin? Why don't they learn how to first say, "Yes" to God? One of the reasons is there's generally more pulpit time devoted to emphasize the weakness of the flesh than the power of righteousness and grace. They hear all the things they "can't do" but never have an understanding of what they "can do" through submission to God. So, let me be one to bring a bit of good news here: You can submit to God. You can resist the devil and live a life that conquers sin. The power to live a life of real change is rooted in your ability to completely surrender to His grace. When you do, here's something you will quickly notice:

When you surrender to God's grace, resistance to sin becomes less of an issue.

Before you "just say no," start by saying, "Yes" to the wonderful life of grace. When you do so, you are positioned to walk not according to your flesh, but according to this grace you have already surrendered to!

#4
KEEP GROWING IN GRACE

Many times throughout this book, you will see me reference this life of grace as a journey. And that's exactly what it is! The steps we have seen in this chapter will produce long-lasting change, but it probably will not happen overnight. That's okay! Start where you are and take one step at a time. Begin to change your belief system. Start seeing God like He is *right now*. Submit your whole life to God and watch the devil flee! You've begun a process known as growing in the grace of God. Not that God's grace is changing—it's been the same since Jesus came and fulfilled all of the Law—but your revelation and knowledge of how to live in His grace will constantly be growing. Once you start walking in the truth of righteousness and grace, here's one thing you will immediately realize: The more you encounter God, the less you *have* to and the more you *want* to!

The more you encounter God, the less you have to and the more you want to!

Many people who have been Believers for a long period of time have asked me, "David, why doesn't God give me a word like He used to when I was a baby Christian?" My answer surprises most of them. I say, "Well, I wouldn't be bothered about it because it's really a sign of maturity." See, when you are young in the Lord, you needed every bit of external confirmation and spiritual development you could find. But, as you grow in God, you will find that you no longer need a spiritual IV. Before long, you will be standing on your own two feet and walking by faith!

Does this mean you will never make any more mistakes? Certainly not. Will you have any more temptations of your flesh? Most assuredly. But, here's the difference. The more you grow, understand, and walk in God's grace, the more you fall in love with Him! And the more you love Him, the more you will want to unashamedly live your life to honor Him! Not because you *have* to . . . but because you *want* to. It's called the power of love, and love is the greatest change agent available to Man.

When my sons were in their pre-teen years, it seemed like I was constantly telling them to brush their teeth, put on deodorant, and comb their hair. Sometimes, I would threaten them within an inch of their lives, but still there were less than favorable results . . . until! Until the day they actually became interested in some girl. All of the sudden, I didn't have to ask them to do anything. As a matter of fact, I would have to kick them out of the bathroom because they spent so much time primping. And as soon as they walked out, you could smell the cheap cologne two blocks away. What was the difference? When they *had to*, it was a task; but when they *wanted to*, they never had to be asked or threatened.

They did it out of love.

This is the exact same principle in your walk with God. The more you know Him, the more you love Him. The more you are formed into His image on the inside of you, the more you become like Him. During your walk of grace, people may not always see who you are on the *outside*, but that can never change who you are on the *inside—righteous, holy, and redeemed!* Keep walking.

Keep growing in the grace God has so lavishly poured out on you. Live in His grace and don't be subject to the Law. Stop beating yourself up every time you stumble, fall, or make a mistake. Let God's Word change your belief system, so you can see who and what you really are in Christ. Stop focusing on what it takes to "qualify" you for God's grace and get a revelation of what Jesus provided for you at the cross! Once you believe that, then start boldly declaring it, and then watch how the revelation builds in your heart. Then, you better watch out . . .

. . . Real, lasting, life-long change is coming your way!

CHAPTER 4

EXTREME MEASURES

To read, comprehend, and apply real life-changing principles is a wonderful path to true freedom. However, another resource which can help and encourage you along your journey are real-life testimonies of God's amazing, delivering grace and power. And, I just so happen to know one—first-hand—which I believe will really shed some light on how and why we should live free of fleshly hang-ups and addictions. Allow me to introduce my good friend, A.J. Zambito.

Over the last few years, I have had the awesome opportunity of knowing A.J. Zambito and his wife, Libby. They are remarkable people of faith and one of the most incredible testimonies of God's saving and delivering grace I have ever heard. There is no way I could describe all of what God has done for this family (I strongly encourage you to pick up the DVD of A.J.'s complete testimony), but one part in particular is an amazing example of how God can use extreme measures to set someone free. As soon as I heard him relay this story, I immediately knew this was a testimony—even though it's very unconventional—that would bring freedom to Christians who still struggle to beat addictions.

Let me warn you; this story might go against the grain of most religious ideology and thinking! But, let me ask you a question. Would you rather live under what religion says you must do to get free (and most likely live in bondage the rest of your life) or have God, by His grace, set you completely free from those things that hold you back from being everything God has made you to be? I think the answer is obvious. Every Christian desires to actually live in the freedom they proclaim is available through Christ. And, as you are about to see, that freedom is real.

Remember how the first step to real change was to transform your belief system? Well, this story might just be a great place to help you start that process. I really believe God will speak to you as you enjoy this remarkable testimony of His delivering grace in action.

A LITTLE BACKGROUND

A.J. Zambito was never considered a church boy. Actually, it was just the opposite. At a very young age, he succumbed to a life that offered money, power, territorial reign, and acceptance—the life of a gangbanger. What he didn't realize was all of the violence, drugs, and lawlessness that would accompany that lifestyle. It didn't take long for A.J. to rise to the position of authority he always dreamed of. To put it mildly, this man was quickly becoming the "king of his hill."

The rise of power and popularity in the gang world brought other vices as well. Small doses of recreational drugs gave way to harder, more addicting narcotics. As a result, A.J quickly became addicted to cocaine which ultimately reached a $300.00 a day mark. His life of addiction drove him to do things he never dreamed he would do. With no remorse or regrets, A.J. did whatever it took to keep building his "kingdom" while at the same time never missing a day of narcotics. He was undoubtedly living the gangster highlife, but at the same time, something else was brewing that he was completely oblivious to.

A.J. was being marked as a representative of God's grace!

THEN, EVERYTHING CHANGED

In the height of his gang glory days, something radically happened to A.J. Zambito. He heard the message of grace and gave his heart to Jesus. A.J.'s life would never, ever be the same. Now, he had another mission in life—his *real* calling—to spread the message of Jesus' love and forgiveness to every single person he could find. And why not start with the ones who knew him the best—the old gangbangers.

So, he did just that.

One day while telling the boys in his gang what had happened in his life, A.J. (not being from a church background) described his conversion like this, "Hey man, the Dude has set me free!" And, yes, he was free indeed. A life of violence and hate was transformed to a heart of compassion and mercy. The $300.00 a day cocaine addiction was instantly gone. What used to be a drive to build A.J.'s kingdom was now a passion to build God's Kingdom. The person standing in front of these gang members might have looked like the old gang leader, but on the inside, A.J. Zambito was a transformed individual.

After witnessing this remarkable change in their former leader, one of his old running buddies said, "Man, we can see you've changed. That's something we might have to try out for ourselves one day." BINGO! That was music to A.J.'s ears! It seemed that taking the risk of going back and sharing his story was paying big dividends. His life-change was undeniable and maybe, just maybe, the power of God's grace and love on display was breaking up some hard, fallow ground. All systems were on go, and progress for the Kingdom was inevitable.

While in the middle of describing his conversion experience, A.J. stepped back a few steps, reached into his shirt pocket, and pulled out a pack of cigarettes. Taking a cigarette out of the pack, he lit it and began to smoke. Knowing there would be some confusion and questioning from the ex-gang members, he quickly looked at them and said, "Well, I can't explain why the Dude set me instantly free from every addiction except cigarettes. I guess He's still working on this one." While he figured his honesty would be well received, the response from listening, interested gang members was not what he expected. Actually, it was heart-wrenching.

While A.J. stood there with a cigarette in his mouth, one of the guys looked at him and spoke these words A.J. will never forget. He said, "Well, I don't know if I can try the Dude or not! Man, I have so much garbage that if He can't set me free from *all of it*, then I don't want *any of it!*" In one instant, and from one seemingly harmless act, every gang member present had a change of heart. Yes, they knew this man who stood in front of them was radically changed. Yes, they knew something or someone caused this transformation to happen. Yet, if God wasn't big enough to set them totally free, then maybe He wasn't the answer they were looking for. And, they turned around and walked away.

Grieved over the magnitude of what just occurred, A.J. reluctantly finished his cigarette.

REALITY CHECK

Now, most Christians would like to think God was condemning him! That God was mad at him and was going to hold him eternally accountable for doing something that turned sinners away from receiving Jesus. But, in reality, that wasn't the case at all. You see, God wasn't judging him; A.J. was condemned in his own heart. And, he knew something had to drastically change.

Returning back to his home, he told his wife (who is also his pastor) all that had happened. Feeling like an opportunity to advance the Kingdom had slipped right through his hands, he said, "Honey, I have to quit smoking. Just look what it caused today." His wife, full of the knowledge of God's grace, looked him in the eye and said, "A.J. you're not ready to quit. Keep smoking!" That's right, his pastor told him to keep smoking!

Now, I know a multitude of Christians who would never believe a pastor would or should tell someone such a thing! As a matter of fact, they would probably think she was the anti-Christ incarnate for having the audacity to tell someone to keep "sinning." But, all I can say is thank God she

That's right, his pastor told him to keep smoking!

understood the grace of God and did not react or respond from the Law. If she did, the eventual outcome would have not been the same because the story does not stop right here.

God's grace was about to be on full display!

SMOKE THESE OR KILL US

Sad to say, A.J. did not heed to his wife's advice. Instead, he just knew that God would and could miraculously deliver him from his addiction to nicotine just like He instantly removed his desire for cocaine. With his tenacious mindset, he did exactly the opposite of what he was encouraged to do and went that same day and threw away all of his cigarettes—every last one of them! Even though this might have been a courageous move, there was one, small issue that A.J. overlooked: His body was not ready for the withdrawals from nicotine!

And things got real ugly, really quick.

For the next few days, this "new creature in Christ" reverted back to some of his old lifestyle. Not having the nicotine his body was so accustomed to, A.J. went on a tirade throughout his entire house. He treated everybody like a dog, cursed his kids, tore up furniture, and even inflicted physical harm to his loving wife. Obviously, this was not the results he had planned on. Everyone he came in contact with could tell he was definitely not "getting free." In fact, it seemed he was in a backwards spiral from just a few days prior.

One day while sitting at his house, just cursing up a storm, A.J.'s wife (also his pastor) walked into his room and gave him a pack of cigarettes which she had purchased for him! That's right. His pastor bought him a pack and threw them at him. She had come to the conclusion that God would rather he smoke than to cause uncontrolled havoc on their entire household and family. Tossing them across the room, she said these words, "A.J, I'm giving you a choice. Either smoke these or kill us all!" Her resolve got his attention, to say the least.

It was obvious that his attempt to walk away from this addiction in his own strength was not working. In fact, it was bringing more pain than freedom. Convicted by his actions and his wife's strength to face the facts, he replied, "Honey, I want to quit smoking so badly. Just look what it is doing to our family." Understanding the fullness of the entire situation, his wife's response was not only full of truth, but covered in the grace of God. She said, "A.J. you're just not ready. You need to quit when God takes it away from you. Smoking is not affecting God. He's not upset with you. He will anoint you just as much whether you are smoking or not! But, this is *definitely* affecting your witness to others. You want to win your old buddies to Christ but this habit is, and will, limit your effectiveness. They see it as a weakness. A.J., smoking is not the issue—your witness is the issue."

> *"Smoking is not the issue—your witness is the issue."*

Oh, thank God for His grace and for those who will speak His truth in love!

SMOKE THOSE . . .

Can you just imagine how liberating it was to hear this truth? Again, most Christians couldn't even fathom the fact of a pastor buying someone a pack of cigarettes let alone taking them the pack and telling them, "Smoke these!" That almost seems like blasphemy. But, the truth was in what this woman of God said: "Smoking is not the issue. Your witness is the issue." Now, A.J. has a greater cause and motivation to stop his habit. Not only does it have a negative effect on his life and family, it has the potential of making his remarkable testimony to no avail for some who sees smoking as a weakness.

Finally, A.J. was on the track to deliverance.

He did, indeed, smoke that pack. But, before he finished all of them, he heard a voice say, "Pick up those last seven cigarettes." Honestly, he thought he was going crazy. Then, the voice continued, "Smoke those and buy no more." Now he knew he was losing his mind! Who in the world would be telling him to do such a thing? It had to be the devil, right? Surely this didn't come from God. He only knew one person who could straighten this out—his wife.

Immediately after hearing these clear, specific directives, A.J. did the perfect thing; he called his wife. When she answered the phone, he told her everything he had just heard and then asked, "Honey, could the Dude be talking to me?" She answered, "Yes, A.J. The voice was God. Do what He told you to do!" After receiving this confirmation, A.J. did in fact follow those specific instructions and gladly finished those last seven cigarettes.

The next day while driving home from his office, another pack of cigarettes fell down from the driver's side visor. Immediately, A.J. remembered what the voice had said, "Smoke those and *buy* no more." Looking at the pack in his lap, he reasoned that he could in fact smoke these because he would not be violating what God had instructed him to do. God said, "Buy no more," and he had not bought this pack since the voice spoke. So, on the trip from his office to the house, A.J. smoked every last cigarette in that pack. Actually, he didn't stop there. Once he got home, he found every pack that was stashed away. And he smoked them all!

And then, God spoke.

"BUY NO MORE"

Finishing his last smoke, A.J. heard the voice of God speak once again. But this time, it was a bit different as God only said, "Buy no more." Notice, God didn't say, "Smoke those," just "Buy no more." Even though he knew God had spoken, this instruction seemed much more difficult to swallow as now there was no provision for flesh. No backup plan. No plan B! This time, there was no outlet to smoke and no justification to continue in this habit. Just the simple directive, "Buy no more!"

Just like the first time the voice spoke, A.J. immediately called his wife for confirmation and consultation. Upon telling her what God had specifically said this time, he quickly confessed, "Honey, I'm scared. What do I do? You know what happened the last time I tried to quit. Would you go buy a pack and hide them from me just in case I go crazy like last time?" Hearing the fear in his voice, his wife simply answered, "A.J., what did God say?" He responded, "Buy no more." She continued, "Then baby, if that's what God said, then He's going to help you through this time. Now if you go and buy some, you will never quit. This time you're not quitting; God is taking them from you."

This sounded like a good plan, but still more questions loomed in A.J.'s mind. He asked, "What if this is not God? What if this is just something in my head? What if I'm just going crazy?" Following these questions, his wife spoke the simple words that would launch A.J. into a life of complete freedom. She said, "A.J., do you love Him?" "Yes," he replied. "Then, do you TRUST Him?" "Yes, I do!" "Then all you have to do is give it a shot. The struggle will not be with your addiction, but with your own fear."

That was the day of total freedom for A.J. Zambito. Through drawing strength from the Word to overcome his own fear, identifying with his new life in Christ, and trusting in God's delivering power, he has never smoked another cigarette from that day on. And today, his witness is stronger than ever and his personal testimony of God's delivering grace is touching the lives of tens of thousands around the world.

The more you fall in love with Him, the less other things have a hold on your life!

Oh, the amazing grace of our God!

TIME FOR THE EXCHANGE

This is the kind of deliverance that God's interested in—real deliverance and real change—from the inside out. Change will never happen by someone beating you over the head, telling you everything that's wrong with you and screaming, "You have to quit doing this." As we saw in the last chapter, real, long-lasting, life-long change comes from a revelation of God's divine love. The more you fall in love with Him, the less other things have a hold on your life.

As remarkable as this truth is, most Christians can't grasp this concept mainly because their "deliverance" came from the Law.

Meaning, they stopped doing what they were involved in out of fear of what would happen if they continued. Of course, as soon as they weren't afraid of the consequences any longer, guess what happened? They went right back to doing what they were "delivered" from. They jumped right back on the Christian merry-go-round of life.

Here's another shift for your thinking: No matter how hard you try, you can't change yourself. If you could, then why would you need the power of grace? Why did Jesus give His life on the cross? What's the use of the Holy Spirit working in you? The good news is while you cannot change within yourself, what you *can do* is EXCHANGE your life for the life of God, by believing on Jesus.

> *...while you cannot change within yourself, what you can do is EXCHANGE your life for the life of God.*

Knowing this truth is it any wonder Paul wrote:

"I have been crucified with Christ; it is no longer I who live, but Christ lives in me; and the life which I now live in the flesh I live by faith in the Son of God, who loved me and gave Himself for me."

Galatians 2:20

This is the greatest trade-off ever known to Mankind. Your sin for His grace. Your unrighteousness for God's righteousness. Your weakness for His strength. Your spiritual death sentence for His eternal life. When will real change occur? When you stop trying to change your life by yourself and exchange it for the life God has provided for you. Sometimes, your freedom might come in an unconventional way or go against the religious way of thinking. That's okay. The real issue is not changing "by the book," but rather getting free to serve God at your maximum capacity.

And that, my friend, is your desired results!

CHAPTER 5

GRACE FROM A KINGDOM PERSPECTIVE

O ver the next few chapters, we are going to embark on a remarkable journey of God's grace—what it is, what it does, and how it functions in our daily lives. And, we're going to start by looking at grace from a Kingdom perspective, or in another words, how God sees it. Before we start, let me give you a quick word of warning: You're probably going to see some areas and functions of grace that you've never seen before OR been told were not true. That's okay. What I challenge you to do is to open your heart and see what God's Word really says. Make your decision that, starting right now, you are not going to vacillate between the Law and grace. It's time to leave the Law behind and go "all in" to God's amazing grace. Do you know why this commitment is important?

Because it only takes one drop of the Law to taint a life in pursuit of grace!

I remember when my boys were younger; we used to eat at restaurants which allowed you to get your own soft drink. My boys would take their cups, head straight to the soda machine, and make what was called a "suicide" drink (Honestly, I never understood that term!). They would start on one end and put in a little bit of Coke®, then a little bit of Sprite®, then Dr. Pepper®, some Diet Coke® and so on, mixing all the flavors until their glass was full. Then, you can only guess what the next step was—"Hey dad, taste this!" And, being a good father, I would drink the dreaded "suicide" drink.

Believe it or not, I started getting used to the taste over the years. With everything blended together, none of the individual colas really stood out, *unless* they added just one, small smidgen of a particular flavor . . . root beer! It wouldn't matter if they had a half-gallon of all the other flavors, it was amazing how a small squirt of root beer permeated the entire drink and everything else lost its effectiveness and flavor. Thankfully, I like root beer—just not mixed with six or seven other flavors!

The "suicide" drink is not only a child's simple concoction; it's also a great example of how grace and the Law cannot mix. You see, every time you learn and develop in God's grace, it's like adding another shot of it into your life's mixture. Revelation is flowing. Freedom is now more than just an unobtainable goal, but rather an actual lifestyle. Things you've wrestled with for years are now not even an issue. Everything is blended well and tasting good until . . . until you turn and add that one drop of the Law—a.k.a. the "spiritual root beer."

Now, everything tastes like that one drop!

For example, look at the Christians who love the Lord and live in grace, but believe they are bound under a curse because their parents went through a divorce. People who succumb to this thinking have let this one drop of the Law contaminate their revelation of God's grace that's at work in their lives. Whether they realize it or not, what they are saying is that their parents' failure is stronger than what Jesus did on the cross! Well, what about the parents who divorced, remarried, and then divorced again? Does that mean their children were cursed, then not cursed, only to be cursed again? Of course not. Yet, many Christians stumble at this one drop of the Law and stay bound to this deception.

Another example is the Believer who has a working knowledge of God's grace in their own life, but still chooses to believe that God is angry at all unbelievers. They just know that "He's just about 'fed up' with all this nonsense here on earth. These sinners are about to get what they deserve!" And then, they don't understand why unbelievers don't respond to their plea of "Come and serve our God—*who is fed up with you*—and then you can be as miserable as we are!" As crazy as this might seem, this happens all the time, and who are the casualties? The scores of people who never experience a saving knowledge of a loving, gracious God.

> *Rejection is never the way to repentance.*

We need to come to an understanding of a very, simple principle: Rejection is never the way to repentance. This is not only true in spiritual matters, either. Just think of the last time the "silent treatment" worked to resolve an issue with your spouse or your children? It probably has never worked! Rejection does not pave the way to reconciliation. The Bible *never* says that the fear of God's judgment or His rejection will draw people to salvation. What the Bible *does* plainly say is:

> *". . . not realizing that God's kindness is intended to lead you toward repentance?"*
>
> **Romans 2:4 (NIV)**

There are countless numbers of examples of how people let one piece of the Law infiltrate their belief system, but the bottom line is this: It's time for a change! Change in the way we think. Change in the way we see God. It's time to shift from religious thinking and begin to understand God's life-changing grace from His point-of-view—the Kingdom perspective!

SOMEONE MOVED IN

One of the most powerful questions any Christian can ask himself is, "Am I serving God for what He can *do* for me OR for what He has already *done* for me?" The honest answer to this question is the beginning of understanding God's grace in action from His perspective. If you are like the ones who serve God for what He's going to do, then guess what? You will live your Christian life running after the latest "blessing," all the while struggling with the weaknesses of your flesh and petty hang-ups that constantly keep you connected to your fallen nature. But, here's another mind shift for you:

You can live both FREE and BLESSED!

It comes down to knowing what God *did* before you pursue what God is going *to do*.

Now, don't get me wrong; I whole-heartedly believe God is a loving Heavenly Father who continuously blesses His children! But if you are only pursuing God for what He's going to do, without a revelation of what He has already done, then your connection with Him is more *external* than *internal*. So, the moment you don't "feel blessed," you immediately begin to rationalize that God has left you high and dry. However, it doesn't have to be that way. There is another depth of communion—an internal relationship—with God that produces far more lasting fruit.

Once again, go back to the day you were born again. Of all the great things that happened to you that day, one thing you might have overlooked is the importance of how God repositioned Himself. Up until the moment you believed and said, "Yes," to Jesus, God was just an external being—someone who lived all around you. But, guess what? The very second the Lord Jesus came to take up residence inside your heart, something else happened as well. The Bible says that Christ is the bodily fullness of the Godhead (Colossians 2:9), which means at that very same instance, God, Himself, instantaneously went from just being *around* you to being *in* you!

An external God suddenly became an internal Heavenly Father.

...you will never live to your full potential in Christ until you have a revelation of Who lives inside of you!

It is so important to grab hold of this truth because you will never live to your full potential in

Christ until you have a revelation of Who lives inside of you! Think about it. Everything that God is—love, mercy, grace, compassion, healing, restoration, etcetera—is now residing *in you*. The "blessing" you seek from an external source is in you . . . every, single day. Jesus said the Kingdom of God is no longer around you, but that "the Kingdom of God is within you." (Luke 17:21) Whether you realize it or not, you now are a living, breathing specimen of God's Kingdom in action.

And a representative of His Kingdom grace.

POWER OF REDEMPTION

One of the most obvious acts of God's grace was when He sent His Son, Jesus, to die for all Mankind. Any natural father who loves his children cannot even start to fathom the sacrifice it would take to send his only child to die in the place of someone else. But before Jesus ever went to the cross, God's grace was already in motion:

> *"But God demonstrates His own love toward us, in that while we were still sinners, Christ died for us."*
>
> **Romans 5:8**

It's one thing to give up your son for someone who might already love you, but to offer him as a sacrifice for a group of people who hate you? Now that's a different level of love. A different level of grace! While we were enemies of God, He willingly put His love on the line and provided not only a way to Heaven, but He also made it possible for us to enjoy some Heaven while here on the earth. Not only did Jesus wash our sins away, but the curse of the Law which once ruled over us was completely destroyed. The Apostle Paul boldly declared it like this:

> *"Christ has redeemed us from the curse of the law, having become a curse for us. . ."*
>
> **Galatians 3:13**

In its root form, the word "redeemed" means *"to purchase"* or *"buy back."* Again, when my boys were small, we spent a good number of days in pizza parlors which had all kinds of video and arcade games. After finishing each game, we would receive a certain amount of tickets, depending upon how well we played. The higher our score, the more tickets we received. At the end of the night, we would gather up all of our winnings and take them to the counter where numerous toys and gadgets awaited our arrival. I would tell the boys, "Guys, let's go *redeem* our tickets for some prizes." Within a few minutes, hundreds of tickets were handed over in exchange for chewing gum, laser lights, stuffed animals, and even a Slinky® or two!

The exact same thing happened over 2000 years ago, but it didn't take place at a pizza parlor! It was on a cross called Calvary. Jesus shed His spotless blood and presented it to the Father and said, *"I'm here to redeem my prize,"* and that prize was you! That prize was me! That prize was all of Mankind who had been subjected and enslaved to the Law. God's grace was not only in action before Christ died, but it was released in full measure when Jesus said, *"It is finished!"* (John 19:30)

While Christ's redemptive work was complete, the age of grace was only beginning.

A DAILY DOSE

So many times I have seen people come to an altar, completely empty themselves into the hands of a loving, compassionate, and merciful God, and walk away with a brand new life in Christ. They knew beyond any shadow of a doubt that the blood of Jesus had washed away their past, and God's grace was on their life. That usually lasted until the following Sunday. It was then some "caring saint" came up and said, "You're a Christian now. It's time to clean up your act!" Every time I would hear these words, something seemed foundationally wrong with this statement. It was this:

Even when our act is cleaned up, it's still an act!

No matter how much you or I try and "clean it up," we will never be good enough in our own flesh to deserve God's righteousness or His presence in our lives. It will still be just an act, or in other words, a failed attempt of looking like we have it all together. It's no more than a show or a masquerade. For young, spiritual babies, this sends a confusing message that the grace which was strong enough last Sunday to make them righteous is not capable of keeping them righteous. The truth is: *God's grace is the ONLY thing that can sustain a daily walk with Him.*

That's exactly why Paul said these words as an encouragement to Believers:

"But where sin abounded, grace abounded much more,"

Romans 5:20

Of course, those who are operating under the Law always camp on the first part of this verse and say, "See, even the Bible says that sin is all around us! You can't get away from it!" Well, it doesn't take a Bible scholar to figure that out. Just look around you every single day. It's blatantly obvious that we live in a fallen, spiritually degenerate world. But, that's not even the focus of Paul's writing in this verse. The emphasis is even though sin and the temptation to sin is everywhere; God's grace to overcome sin is much more plentiful and abounding. It all depends on what has your focus—sin or grace.

Aren't you glad that Paul didn't say that where sin is overflowing, our ability to defeat it just has to be stronger? If that was the case, we would ALL be in trouble! Are you going to have troubles in life? Yes. Learn from them. Will there be trials? Yes.

> *God's grace to overcome sin is much more plentiful and abounding!*

Grow through them. Will temptations to sin come? Absolutely. Get stronger as you overcome them. The truth from God's Word is that sin is looming, but praise God, there is something *living in you* that supersedes the power of sin . . .

. . . God's powerful, sustaining grace!

THE TWO ARE NOT THE SAME

To help you start seeing how grace to overcome sin works from God's perspective, I want to explain the difference between two terms which, in some ways sound synonymous, but in reality are different. They are the words "godly" and "God-like." Many times, people think living "godly" and "God-like" is the same, but they both carry unique qualities. Let's take a look at how they differ and where every New Testament Believer needs to be:

> **Godly.** Living godly is when you try to pattern your life like God. It's the term people use to describe their attempt at living a good Christian life. Think about how many times you've heard people say, "Pray for me. I'm trying to live as godly as I possibly can." Even though their heart and intentions might have been right and this sounds like the right thing a Christian should say, can you see the basic flaw with this statement? It's all about what *they* are trying to *do*.

As I said earlier, trying to live the perfect, righteous, godly life is not hard—it's impossible! If you don't believe me, just look at the people who lived under the Old Covenant. Their only hope of being righteous was completely dependent on what they did—fulfill and keep the whole Law. The problem was they always came up short. The same is true today. As long as you try to do all the "right" things, failure will be your outcome and frustration will be your ill-wanted friend. As soon as you blow it (and you will) all of a sudden, you will be labeled as "ungodly" as quickly as you were called "godly."

...trying to live the perfect, righteous, godly life is not hard—it's impossible!

Now, should Christians, who are the demonstration of God on the earth, represent Him well? Absolutely. Should we conduct our relationships and affairs on earth in a way He would be proud? Yes.

But, the way to accomplish this is through His grace rather than through our works. It's when we live God-like.

God-like. To live God-like is different than living godly in the fact that being God-like is the pursuit to understand the character and nature of God Himself. One thing that Law-minded Christians seem to forget is how Genesis 1:26-27 describe how we were made—in God's *likeness* and in His *image*. What this means is that we were created to be just like God! His nature lives on the inside of us. His characteristics are woven into our very being and fiber. So, since we are made God-like, why don't we act more like Him? The answer is surprisingly simple: Religion doesn't allow anyone to live how they were created—like God!

Religion keeps you toiling and working, trying to obtain the best, godly life you possibly can. But the truth is you don't have to work to be what you already are! The issue is that far too many Christians don't realize how they were created in the first place. They are still stuck in the mindset that says, "You are a rotten, low-down, dirty sinner with no ability to ever be godly." But when you begin to get the revelation of what the Bible says—that you were created just like God—then the concept of living godly becomes second-nature.

Are you ready for another shift in your thinking? Here it is: When you discover how you were originally created in His image, then living godly becomes the outflow of being God-like! It's nothing you have to work up or strive for; you can live godly simply because it's in your nature to do so. Paul described it this way:

"For the grace of God that brings salvation has appeared to all men, teaching us that, denying ungodliness and worldly lusts, we should live soberly, righteously, and godly in the present age,"

Titus 2:11-12

> *God's grace does not make you lawless or give you the freedom to live ungodly!*

Do you see what teaches us to deny all ungodliness? Is it religion? Is it the works of our flesh? Is it how much we try to live godly and do all the "right things?" No, none of these things! Paul says that one thing—and one thing only—has the power and the capability to teach us how to deny all ungodliness: God's grace! The truth and power of this scripture is:

When we discover and live in God's grace then we will not adhere to anything that removes or taints our God-likeness.

Contrary to what some people believe, God's grace does not make you lawless or give you the freedom to live ungodly. It's quite the opposite. God's grace teaches you to deny ungodliness and live like you were originally created—in HIS image and likeness. God-likeness makes godliness the "norm" and not the exception. What's the key? Learning who you are, how you were created, and living like God originally designed. When you begin to wholeheartedly pursue God-likeness, godliness is the natural product.

"OPEN MY EYES"

Before I had a revelation of being God-like, I found myself praying things like, "Lord, open the eyes of my heart so I can see You and be more like You." I prayed this day after day after day. Then one day I felt the Lord stop me right in the middle of my prayer and say, "David, stop asking me to make you more like I've already made you!" I had to stop and think about that for a moment, but then I knew exactly what He meant:

What I was praying for was already in me.

All the time I was working to be godly, I never realized I was already God-like. Like most Christians, I was searching for something on the *outside* to help me be a better Christian on the *inside*. But that day, everything changed. In my life, God moved from *external* to *internal*. This revelation changed my prayer from "God, make me more like You" to "God, help me to *believe* that I am becoming more of what You have already made me to be!" I had a shift in my thinking, and I never saw myself the same way again. My belief system changed to line up with what God said about me.

Did I still have flaws in my life? Sure, but I knew that . . . *in Him* . . . I was flawless. With all of my incompleteness, I knew I was complete . . . *in Him!* There was no mistaking my unrighteousness (the Church told me every Sunday how unrighteous I was.), but now I knew I was righteous . . . *in Him!* And guess what? If you are a new creation in Christ, you have the exact same testimony! In Him you are flawless, complete, and righteous. Now, it's time to walk in this new life of freedom and grace. Not just for you . . .

. . . But for those around you.

EARTH-TO-EARTH

The power of redemption and the sustenance of your daily walk are marvelous examples of God's grace extended from Heaven to Earth. But, have you ever stopped to realize that there is another dimension of grace in the Kingdom of God? It's not Heaven-to-Earth, but rather Earth-to-Earth. It's not just God's grace *towards* you, but His grace *through* you, freely given to other people.

Think about this. What good would it be for you to have the love and grace of God in your spiritual DNA, but you never loved a single person? What's the benefit of living with God's compassion on the inside of you, but you're always judgmental, critical, and inconsiderate to everyone around you? Why would you accept God's grace for your own life but nail everyone else to the cross for every little thing they did "wrong?" Friend, the next step of grace, from the Kingdom perspective, is showing a lost and dying world not how "wrong" they are, but how righteous they can be in Christ!

Allow me to let you in on a little secret. Are you ready? Christians who still live under the principles of the Law have personal hang-ups and blow it. Surprised? You shouldn't be. But, guess what? *So do people who live under grace!* It doesn't make any difference if you live under the rules and regulations of the Law or the freedom of grace; no one is exempt from sin. No one! The issue is not whether people sin or not; the issue is how you respond to sin not only in your life, but in the lives of those around you. The grace you show to others is a real meter of where you are in your journey.

The way you respond to people's mess ups is directly connected to two things: How much revelation you are walking in concerning God's grace and how much you know the character and heart of God. To really see grace from the full, Kingdom perspective, both of these elements need to be constantly developing. And there's only one way to see exactly where you are in the process.

When people fall into sin.

Here's something to be prepared for. When you start to understand God's grace, grow in grace, and walk in grace, don't be surprised if you begin to notice every little flaw in yourself and others. It's a test to see where you are. Think about it. How else will you know if you are learning to live in God's grace if you never come across anything that requires a response of grace? It's like a doctor who practices medicine. How will they ever know if their prescriptions work unless someone who is ill takes the medicine and responds favorably? When you can actually see someone else fall into sin or struggle with an addiction and *respond like God*, then you know you are on your way to living the Kingdom grace life.

THE ONLY ONES THEY SEE

There was a song many years ago that said, "You're the only Jesus some will ever see." How true this statement is, and even more-so today. With that thought in mind, how critical is it for us to know the real Jesus? Jesus, the Healer. Jesus, the Redeemer. Jesus, the One who meets needs. Jesus, the merciful Savior. Jesus, gracious Lord. Jesus, the radiance of God's glory and the exact representation of His being. (Hebrews 1:3) Jesus, full of mercy and grace.

Friend, THAT'S the Jesus this world is longing to know . . . and that Jesus lives in you, right now! I like to say it this way:

The God you <u>know</u> is the God you'll <u>show</u> to others.

This Kingdom life of grace is three-fold: grace for redemption, grace to live powerfully over sin, and grace to extend to others. It's time to understand who you are, how you were made, the grace that is available to you on a daily basis, and the power you have to show God's grace to others. Why not determine right now to be "all in?" Decide that, from this day on, you and your house are going to serve the God of grace and not be ruled by religion any longer. Let the light of the Gospel be spread to every single person you come in contact with. Start living as God lives, believing like God believes, seeing what God sees, and walking in the abounding grace of God . . .

. . . For His Kingdom and His glory!

CHAPTER 6

THE POWER OF GRACE

My journey to understand, live, and teach God's grace really kicked into high gear a few years ago. Up until that point, I had always preached and led people to a saving knowledge of Jesus (which happens more today than ever), but lacked the revelation to teach them how to live free and not live a frustrated Christian life. Then, the revelation of the power of grace began to overtake me. For a number of months, it seemed like everything that came out of my mouth was completely encompassed by God's grace. If I would preach on the rapture, God's grace would be included. Messages on family life would wind up being about God's grace. Even messages about tithing and stewardship ended up with grace! I even tried to preach "hellfire and brimstone," but guess what came out?

God's amazing, unexplainable, supernatural grace.

I just *knew* everyone who heard this message of grace would have the same fervor and receptivity as I did. Not so! As a matter of fact, I had to go back and re-read John 8:32 to make sure Jesus didn't say, "You shall know the truth and the truth shall make you *mad*," because, at times, this message made more people mad than free. But, it didn't matter. I knew what God was revealing and releasing into my spirit, and I couldn't stop—and will never stop—preaching on the power of God's overwhelming grace.

One day while in prayer, the Lord spoke to my heart and said, "David, the day you preach grace so strong that everybody accuses you of giving people a 'license to sin,' you'll be close to preaching it right!" At that moment, I thought to myself, "I have a long way to go." And by His grace and His anointing, this message of the Gospel is now being heralded around the world . . .

. . . With signs of freedom following.

THE TRUTH SETS YOU FREE

There really is no way to write a book or live a life of grace without addressing some myths which religious-minded people have made vastly popular. Actually, those who are caught up in religion more than having a relationship with God would not have much ground to stand on if these ideologies were actually true. The problem is that the people who actually believe these things never seem to get free and live in their God-likeness. Instead, they seem satisfied to go through the motions of Christianity but never break the chains of religion and the flesh. Is it any wonder the Bible says that people perish because of their lack of knowledge? (Hosea 4:6)

So, let's look at a few misconceptions of grace and see the truth of God's Word. For it is the *truth*—not religious jargon—that will set you free. I say, "Let freedom reign!" Let's live in grace!

RELIGION SAYS:
Grace is just a license to sin whenever you want to.

THE TRUTH IS:
Grace gives you the freedom to confront issues and get free from them!

This seems to be one of the most popular theories about God's grace—that you can go hog-wild in the flesh, sin all you want to, and still just "live on grace." In all actuality, most people I have found who really believe this (and teach it to others) have one thing in common: they, themselves, are dealing with major sin issues and weaknesses of their own flesh. Those who seem to constantly harp on particular issues of the flesh are usually, unknowingly revealing their own inner-personal battles. Then what happens when the "hard-line" preacher has sin revealed? The grace they once ridiculed is now the grace they call upon for restoration.

But, it doesn't have to be that way.

The understanding of God's grace is the power for any Believer to live a life of freedom in Jesus. Hear me carefully: Grace is not a license to sin, but rather it is the freedom to bring out your weaknesses and be delivered from them! I like to say it this way:

Grace doesn't free you to do what you want to do; it frees you from the desire to want to do!

In other words, living in the power of grace takes away your "want to." When you begin to understand God's marvelous grace, forgiveness, mercy, and love, why in the world would you *willingly* want to do anything to abuse or compromise them? If God so graciously sent His Son to purchase you from the slavery of sin and redeem you from the curse of the Law, then why would you give any foothold to the very things Jesus gave His life to deliver you from? Why would anyone abuse what has been so freely provided? When you see what Jesus did on the cross and the price He paid for your freedom, your attitude towards sin and grace becomes like the Apostle Paul when he said:

> *"I have been crucified with Christ . . . Therefore, I do not treat God's gracious gift as something of minor importance and defeat its very purpose; I do not set aside and invalidate and frustrate and nullify the grace (unmerited favor) of God."*
>
> **Galatians 2:20a ,21a (AMP)**

One of the key factors that can keep you more Law-minded than grace-minded boils down to which one you're exposed to. The truth is, if you hear something long enough—whether it's grace or the Law—you will eventually believe it to be so. Many years ago, the computer industry coined a termed "GIGO" which simply meant: "Garbage In/Garbage Out!" With that term in mind, what happens when you infiltrate yourself with the Law? You keep sinning. The more you hear about the Law, the more you will find yourself dealing with sin AND trying to hide it (which is more dangerous than dealing with it openly). If you are constantly hearing what the Law says you "*can't do,*" more than likely, you will wind up participating in those exact things! That's true even in the natural. Just leave your house and tell your child, "While I'm gone, you can have any food in the house, but just don't touch those cookies." More than likely, when you return, a cookie will be missing.

I knew a youth pastor who was on staff at the same church for over six years. During that time, he never dedicated much time on the sin of premarital sex. Instead, he constantly preached to his youth what they "could do" in Jesus. The results? In six years and with over 400 teens in attendance each week, not one teenage girl became pregnant. NO, NOT ONE! When he left that particular assignment, his successor took a different route. This new youth pastor immediately began to preach, week after week, about sex, lust, and why you "can't do that until you're married." The results? Within 18 months, there were so many babies born (from teens in the group) that they had to start offering a nursery and a nursing moms room for each *youth* service! You see, the Bible is true:

Signs follow that which is preached!

Just think about what would happen if you exclusively fed on what the Bible says you "*can do*," in Jesus. Signs would follow those words and those thoughts! I'm a living testimony that when you begin to focus on the grace of God—who God says you are, what God says you can have, and all you can do in Christ—the desire to sin will begin to dissipate. I like to say it like this: Learning what *He did* is more powerful than hearing what *you can't do*! It's the power of knowing God's grace and . . .

Learning what He did is more powerful than hearing what you can't do!

. . . Grace gives you the freedom to conquer and live *above* sin!

RELIGION SAYS:
Grace is something you have to work for and earn.

THE TRUTH IS:
Grace is a free gift Jesus provided at the cross.

One of the favorite words in the religious world is "work." You have to "work" to keep your salvation, "work" for your righteousness. If you "work" and do enough "good things," then God will someway, somehow, look beyond your awful sin and grant you a drop of grace when you need it! It's funny how this mentality closely resembles manual labor—if you don't work, then you don't earn. But, spiritual truths and the principles of labor on this earth can rarely be related or compared to one another.

Thank God!

When you read the New Testament, you will find what Jesus said about laboring and working in your Christian walk. If you've been working to earn God's grace, get ready . . . this might surprise you! After hearing the teachings and seeing the miracles of Jesus, the disciples asked what they had to do, or what work was required of them, to do the works of God? Jesus answered and said:

> *"This is the work of God, that you believe in Him whom He sent."*
>
> **John 6:29**

Do you see a word in this scripture that has been the theme of this entire book? The only work that Jesus Himself requires of Believers is this: *to believe!* Now, some religious folks will say, "Well, it can't be that easy. That's not all Jesus meant. He talked about labor and work in other passages of Scripture." And, yes, He did. As a matter of fact, Jesus was the One who said these words:

> *"Come to Me, all you who labor and are heavy laden, and I will give you rest. Take My yoke upon you and learn from Me, for I am gentle and lowly in heart, and you will find rest for your souls. For My yoke is easy and My burden is light."*

> **Matthew 11:28-30**

There it is again! If you are spinning your wheels working and laboring to "earn" something from God, then Jesus simply says, "Stop, believe on Me, and rest." For me, the hardest lesson I've ever had to learn in my Christian walk was how to really rest in God and completely rely on His grace. Once I did, my life completely changed. The same will happen to you. Learning to enter into rest changes you from the mentality of "I have to watch my every step" to "Oh, what a gracious, wonderful, marvelous Savior I serve!"

Do you know what takes a lot of work? *Always trying to do good!* It's amazing how many Christians constantly strive, labor, and toil to "do the right thing" and "resist temptation" in their own flesh and ability with very little results. Just think about how many times you have asked someone (or you've been asked) how a certain part of their life was going, and they said, "Oh, I'm working on it. Keep praying for me." I have news for you: No matter how much you or anyone else prays, you can never "work" enough to overcome the flesh! Without a submitted heart to God, a revelation of the power of grace, and a heart that's full of belief, frustration will always be the normal way of life.

> *Without a revelation of the power of grace, frustration will always be the normal way of life.*

Something else that takes a lot of work is trying to hide a life of sin. The man who continually lies to his wife and co-workers about "working late" and has to constantly track his steps to carry on in an adulterous relationship—that's work! The woman who is addicted to prescription drugs yet has to hide them and tells her children and husband that she's just "tired from the day's activities"—that's work! The teenager who cannot pass up any opportunity to wander through pornographic websites and always hides their laptops or continually deletes their computer's history—that's work! It takes more work to live a life of sin than it does to live a life of grace.

One of the classic descriptions of the word grace is "unmerited favor." I've always loved that portrayal of grace; but honestly, I didn't grab the entirety of what that term meant for many years. One day, I began to see some other words for "unmerited." Words like "undeserved," "unwarranted," and my favorite, *"unearned."* Just like salvation, you or I did nothing to earn it; Jesus paid the entire price—*in full!* Well, since salvation was a free gift, why do we so quickly revert to having to "earn" God's grace, mercy, and favor? The truth is, just as salvation was given to us freely, so is God's grace now unmerited, undeserved, and unearned. What are our requirements to receive His grace?

Believe and rest!

RELIGION SAYS:
You can be disqualified from God's grace.

GOD SAYS:
"My grace is sufficient for you!"
(2 Corinthians 12:9)

Many years ago, I was drawn from a hard-line Pentecostal denomination to what was then developing as the new Charismatic movement. The things I heard coming out of that camp at that time were life to my spirit. Things like "I can do all things through Christ," "I'm the head and not the tail, above only and not beneath," and "I am the righteousness of God in Christ" riveted my soul. The confession and daily application of these and many other truths of God's Word drew my attention. I remember so vividly thinking, "Finally, some other preachers who believe the Bible like I do!" It was a wonderful, new beginning.

Some years later, things in this same camp began to shift. Quite honestly, even though the Charismatic movement has some wonderful men and women of God associated with it, their emphasis seemed to have changed over the years. What used to be "I AM the righteousness of God" somehow dissolved to "You have to make sure you're QUALIFIED for the righteousness of God!" The problem with this is the primary focus had, once again, changed from what *Jesus did* to what people *are doing*!

This mindset is not exclusive with the Charismatic movement. As a matter of fact, MOST Christians—and even whole denominations—still believe and preach that God's grace is on some type of rationing system that has a very limited supply. To me, I can't think of anything more ridiculous than this entire theology! What makes it even more foolish is, according to *Vine's Expository Dictionary of*

New Testament Words, the root word for "Charismatic," *charis* means "accepted, favored," and (you guessed it!) . . .

. . . "Grace."

One thing to always remember is while God's grace—just like His love—is unconditional and everlasting, man's grace—and love—is conditional and most of the time restrictive to what the human brain and emotions are capable of processing. For those who have been labeled as "disqualified" for grace, their grace-chain towards others is a little longer, while others are quick to cut people off and "disqualify" them from God's unchanging grace because of some "wrong thing" they have done. In essence, what this whole idea says is: The weakness of your flesh is more powerful than Jesus' blood that was shed on the cross! Looking at it in this perspective, you can see just how crazy the entire idea of being "disqualified" from God's grace really is.

If you have trouble believing me, then just go to the Bible! My goodness, the Bible is full of individuals who, if they lived in today's world, would be blackballed and marked as being "trouble," "unworthy," and "disqualified" to live in the grace of Almighty God. Just look at a few of these examples:

- **Moses:** "disqualified" by evading the call of God and killing an innocent man in the process. Yet, God chose him to single-handedly lead over two million Israelites out of Egypt's bondage.

- **Abraham:** "ineligible" because he lied about his wife being his sister. Not once, twice, but on three occasions! His outcome? He became the Father of faith with an everlasting covenant with God that we, today, are heirs to!

- **David:** missed the marked by being a liar, a murderer, and an adulterer. Thank God His grace does not live by the "three strikes, you're out" rule! David would have had no hope. Instead, the Bible records David as one the greatest kings and leaders to ever lived, not to mention one of the greatest men of God in all of history.

- **Rahab:** a prostitute became the lineage from which Jesus was brought to the earth! And, she is mentioned in the Hall of Fame of Faith. (Hebrews chapter 11)

- **Jacob:** the very meaning of his name is "deceiver." He won his older brother's birthright unlawfully by deceit and craftiness. But, when it was all said and done, God changed his name into one you might just recognize: Israel!

- **Peter:** a liar and a coward who was full of anger and had an unmanageable temper, fell to the pressure of a young, teenage girl and denounced the very Savior who had just given His life for him. Fifty days later, God chooses this man to stand and preach the first message after Jesus' ascension into Heaven. The results? Three thousand people were saved!

- **Paul:** an assassin, paid by his government to carry out one primary goal: kill Christians! But, God had other plans. After his remarkable transformation, God changed his name from Saul to Paul and his heart from persecutor to an apostle of the Gospel of Jesus. He then wrote two-thirds of the New Testament that you and I read today!

I don't know about you, but I'm sure glad these great patriarchs of faith didn't live in our generation. Why? Because religion would have never given them a chance to be all God had destined them to be! They would have been tarred-and-feathered by most Christians and probably would not have risen to the greatness that lived inside them.

Here's another mind shift for you: If *something* or *someone* can "disqualify" you from the grace of God, it must mean that *someone* or *something* was needed to "qualify" you in the first place. How ridiculous is that? The truth is you and I only needed one thing to qualify for the everlasting grace of God: *the spotless blood of the Lord Jesus!* He paid the price that we might go free. He laid down His life to give us everlasting life. Everything needed to meet the criteria for God's grace was completely met—in full—when Jesus proclaimed, "It is finished!" Notice the last word, "finished." Complete! Done! All requirements are met! Everybody qualifies.

Let me make one very important observation here. I've had some people ask me, "Doesn't the Bible say that we will be disqualified if we don't do 'good'?" Yes, Paul mentions this word "disqualified" several times in the New Testament, but in a different context than most people think. Here is one example:

> *"But I discipline my body and bring it into subjection, lest, when I have preached to others, I myself should become disqualified."*
>
> **1 Corinthians 9:27**

Every time in the New Testament Paul mentions this word, the context of the scripture never says you are unworthy to receive God's gift of grace. (Also see 2 Corinthians 13:5-7 and Titus 1:16.) However, what the Bible does say is that through acts of disobedience, you can limit your effectiveness and witness to those around you. My friend, A.J. Zambito, is a perfect example of this principle. While A.J. was sharing his testimony with that gang member, was he any less saved the moment he took a drag of his cigarette? No, he wasn't. It didn't make any difference to God if A. J. smoked or not! What it *did* affect was his witness. Remember the gang member's response? "If God can't fix it all, then He can't fix any of it." Do we need any more motivation to live God-like? When we do, lost people all around us see the One, true, and living God in action!

Friend, let me strongly encourage you to never, ever let anyone convince you that God's grace is rationed to only those who "deserve it." Be cautious of those who, by their own set of standards, want to disqualify you from God's grace. Many times, these "well-meaning" people have their own, manipulative agendas. Remember, no one's opinion or set of standards and rules qualified you to begin with. To believe that the weakness of your flesh or an act of disobedience nullifies the grace of God for your life is simply not true. His grace is unlimited, unending, all-sufficient, all-powerful, and everlasting.

Learn to live in that grace!

RELIGION SAYS:
You get what you deserve.

THE TRUTH IS:
Grace declares you "Not guilty!"

Have you ever been accused of doing something wrong? Worse yet, have you been accused of something that you actually did do? I think everyone could answer, "Yes" to either or both of these questions. It's not a good feeling to be accused of something you really did, but it's worse for someone to throw accusations toward you for something you didn't do! It's the same way spiritually, as well.

We've already seen how Revelation 12:11 clearly says that Christians have an accuser—the devil. Just one verse before, we also see how extremely persistent he is at his job. The Bible says, he *"accused them* (Christians) *before our God day and night."* (Revelation 12:10) Now, I don't know about you, but over the course of my life, the devil has done his job quite well! Not only has he lived up to his full potential in bringing my faults and failures before the Throne of God, he's also outdone himself by making sure those here on earth have plenty of ammunition to fire my way, as well.

And the religious crowd has jumped on his bandwagon.

But, thanks be to God, I (and hopefully you) have been set free from what the devil and religion thinks and says about me. If the thought of "we get what we deserve" was really true, guess what each and everyone one of us would get? Death! That's what we deserve for our sins, shortcomings, and failures. But, God had another plan—a way of escape and an eternal ransom for the sins of the world.

Jesus, our Messiah!

Ever since I was a teenager, I have always been enthralled by our judicial system and how the legal process works in America. Actually, if I hadn't been called to preach the Gospel, I'm sure I would have pursued practicing law as a career—maybe that's why I love to watch Court TV® so much! Even though there are many details about the law that I still do not know, there is one thing I am fairly versed on: the clause of double jeopardy.

In short, the clause of double jeopardy prohibits someone from being tried twice for the same offense *and* forbids multiple punishments for the same crime. Once someone has been convicted and served the appropriate punishment, another person—even if they are guilty—cannot be tried or sentenced for the same offense. In the United States, this clause is protected by the Fifth Amendment of U. S. Constitution; however, in the spirit world, this law was set into motion over 2,000 years ago . . .

. . . When Jesus died on the cross!

In the spiritual courtroom, you and I have committed crimes, broken the Law, and *deserve* the corresponding punishment—death. The prosecution against us (the devil) not only accuses us himself, but also brings many witnesses to the stand to build the case against us. In the end, the case is clear—Mankind is guilty as charged and deserves the sentence. But, hold on just a minute! This case is not as open-and-closed as it may seem. There is a missing piece of evidence!

The truth is we all have sinned, broken spiritual laws, and committed spiritual crimes that are punishable by death under the Law. The evidence is overwhelming. But, we have an Advocate, a defense attorney. (1 John 2:1) His name is Jesus! Not only is He the One who pleads our case, but He also upholds a vital piece of the law in order to overthrow our conviction—*the clause of double jeopardy*. Yes, by legal standards, we are guilty, but the price has already been paid for our crime. The punishment has already been served—in full—by the One who took our shame, carried our burdens, and paid for all of our sin! The Bible says that Jesus:

". . . entered the Most Holy Place once for all, having obtained eternal redemption."

Hebrews 9:12b

Oh, hallelujah, Jesus paid it all! All of our sin, all of our shame, all of our crimes—they all have been paid for . . . *once and for all.* Every sin you have ever done—paid! Every sin you will ever do—paid! Religion will try to keep you bound to your sin. Tradition will make every attempt to make sure you are constantly aware of what you have done wrong. But, GRACE says, "No, wait a minute! The charges are correct, but he can go free!" Now, like the Apostle Paul, we can declare:

> *All of our sin, all of our shame, all of our crimes—they all have been paid for . . . once and for all.*

"It is for freedom that Christ has set us free."

Galatians 5:1 (NIV)

LIVE IN THIS GRACE

Aren't you glad that grace is the power that takes away your "want to" desire for sin? Thank God His grace is unmerited, unearned, and free to everyone who believes! Isn't it a joy to know that the weakness of your flesh can never disqualify you from God's grace? And thank God you didn't get "what you deserved," but grace boldly pronounces you "not guilty." Can you see now why it is so easy to fall in love with Jesus and live your life for no other purpose but to honor and glorify Him?

Freedom you didn't deserve. Forgiveness you never paid for or had to earn. The liberty to walk above sin and make it your slave.

A bountiful supply of God's mercy that can never be exhausted by the mistakes you make. Friend, this is the power of knowing God's amazing grace! Now, let's start to learn how you walk in this grace and enjoy the life God has already provided.

It's time to be the real you!

CHAPTER 7

FREE TO BE THE REAL YOU

Everywhere you turn nowadays, people are on a quest to find their true identity. I've heard so many people say, "I'm looking for the real me," or "I just need to find myself," and sadly, some take an entire lifetime and go to incredible measures to discover who they really are or are not. I've watched husbands and wives move their entire families across the country or to other parts of the world in search of their "true identity." Maybe they figured if they woke up in a different place, in a different time, they would become different people! But the high majority of the time, relocation didn't produce the answers or revelation they craved; it just cost a bunch of money and wasted a bunch of valuable time. Their quest continued.

Now, you would think that born again Believers would not be lumped into the same pile as those who do not know the Lord and are looking for their real self. One would suppose that since someone has come into the family of God, they would automatically know who they are, what they are, and live their life as the new creation God has made them. Right? Wrong! What's even more heartbreaking than to watch people in the world waste their life in pursuit of their true identity is to see Christians live bound to a religious set of rules rather than fully operate in God's grace! They serve God more out of a fear of going to hell rather than a deep, sincere love to please their Heavenly Father. What's the main reason for this type of mindset? It's simple:

We have an identity crisis in the Body of Christ!

However, by God's grace, that is about to change!

For many years, I've made the statement that it is better for people to not go to church than to go to one that is full of religion. Of course, many people gasp when they hear me say that, but I really believe this to be true. So many people who are under the teachings of the Law more than grace become frustrated, disheartened, and sometimes flat-out mean people! Honestly, I don't blame them. Who wants to live a life that is so regulated and dominated by the Law that it prevents them from living the abundant life Jesus came and gave His life for? The truth is, they don't . . . *you don't* . . . have to live that way. Jesus came to set you free to live and be all He has created you to be in the power of His grace!

And it all starts by knowing who you *were* and who you *are* in Him.

WHO YOU WERE

In their quest for true identity, many people spend countless hours and money tracing their natural heritage and lineage back as far as possible. They want to know who their great-great-great-great-great grandparents were, and just as importantly, what they did! Knowing these facts seem to make the mission of true identity more real and creditable.

Actually, the same thing is true spiritually. One of the reasons we have such an identity crisis in the Body of Christ is because most Christians never understand from where they came. So, for you to see where you are now and to walk in the freedom God has given you today, let's go back and see what is in your spiritual lineage. And when I say go back, I mean go back . . .

. . . All the way to Adam!

To move forward in faith and to see what you *are* in Christ, you must first understand what you *were* in Adam. The comparisons of these two vastly different positions—in Adam and in Christ—do, in some respects, have many of the same principles at work. Let's start by taking a look at what Adam brought into this world.

> *"Therefore, just as through one man sin entered the world, and death through sin, and thus death spread to all men, because all sinned . . ."*
>
> **Romans 5:12**

How does this verse affect you? Well, according to this scripture, every single person who has ever or will ever live on this earth is born into a sinful, fallen, Adamic nature. Think about every newborn you have ever seen. They were so precious, so lovely, and almost angelic (especially if it was your child or grandchild). There they were, maybe just a few hours or days old, when you first laid your eyes on that bundle of joy and persona of peace. Thinking back, did that new baby look like a sinner to you? Did he/she have the similarities of someone who had done awful things and were condemned by their actions? Of course not. They were practically perfect in every way! But, the real truth is . . .

. . . Every baby born into this world is a sinner by the Adamic nature!

You might be scratching your head trying to rationalize this by saying, "Wait a minute, how can those little babies, just hours old, be sinners? They have never committed one sin!" *And you are exactly right.* They were not sinners because of their sinful deeds; however, they were sinners by what they were born in to—a fallen, sinful nature. A person who has never committed one sinful deed is still a sinner without Jesus.

> *A person who has never committed one sinful deed is still a sinner without Jesus.*

Now, fast-forward to the coming of the "last Adam."

WHO YOU ARE

The Bible calls Jesus the "last Adam" (1 Corinthians 15:45) which simply means, just as Adam was the first man through whom sin entered the world, Jesus was sent from Heaven to offer the redemption of all Mankind back to God. Paul continues to describe Adam and Jesus like this:

"But the free gift is not like the offense. For if by the one man's offense many died, much more the grace of God and the gift by the grace of the one Man, Jesus Christ, abounded to many."

Romans 5:15

Isn't it good to know that while you and I were completely messed up, God took care of it? The Bible says that while we were sinners—by our sinful, Adamic nature—God showed His love for us and sent His Son, Jesus to redeem us from the Fall. What a wonderful Savior we serve! And what was the motivating factor for God to send His Son? His grace! His grace is more than enough, more than sufficient to cancel the debt of sin and unrighteousness. And while this new life in Christ is a far superior life than the life in Adam, there are remarkable similarities. Here are a few:

- You were born in Adam. You were born again in Christ.

- In Adam you were a sinner. In Christ you are the righteousness of God.

- You were a sinner without "doing" one sinful deed. You are righteous by what you believe, not by "doing" righteous deeds.

Can you see the resemblance? Just as the offense of sin came on you, the free gift of righteousness came the exact same way! I like to say it this way:

Sin came because Adam blew it, but
righteousness came because Jesus fixed it.

Religious-minded people have always had it in their heads that we don't have to do one single thing to be a sinner, but to be righteous we must do everything right. That's wrong theology! Here's a great mind shift for you: What did you do to become a "sinner?" Nothing! Adam did it for you. In the same light, what did you do to become "righteous?" Nothing! Jesus did it for you. The second you believed on Jesus and you were born again, in that instance, you were "right before God" even though you had never done any righteous deeds!

...you didn't do anything to be a sinner or to be righteous—you simply changed residences!

On that day, whether you knew it or not, you had a change of identity.

WHAT REALLY HAPPENED

In reality, you didn't do anything to be a sinner or to be righteous—you simply changed residences! That day, you walked away from who you were in Adam and started your brand new life in Christ. The Bible says it like this:

"Therefore, if anyone is in Christ, he is a new creation; old things have passed away; behold, all things have become new."

2 Corinthians 5:17

Now, let me expound a bit on this verse. Many Christians believe that the day they got saved is when they became a new creature. Experientially—yes, providentially—no. Jump back over 2000 years ago to a place called Calvary. This was the place where Jesus, the second Adam, gave His life, shed His blood, and became the path back to God that Adam had destroyed. On that day, *at that moment in time,* you and I along with all Mankind became a new creature. Think about it. Did Jesus do anything extra-special the day you believed? No. Was there another step in the process of redemption required from Him for you to become a Christian? No. Did God put you on a waiting list, expecting another act of redemption to buy your freedom from sin? No. The old song we used to sing in church was in fact completely true:

Jesus Paid it All!

When Jesus died on the cross, all of the requirements to take away your sin were met. All obligations fulfilled. The price was paid, the debt of sin was retired, and the "last Adam" had completed His divine mission on earth. On that glorious day, in that very moment, every person providentially became born again. That's right . . . *every, single person who has ever lived on this planet.* What this means is on the day you (or anyone else) got saved, you really didn't become a new creature, instead . . .

. . . You recognized and identified with the new creature you had become the day Jesus died!

That day, you changed to your true identity in Christ. Now, it's time to say "Goodbye" to everything you were in Adam.

THE NEW YOU

I can remember when growing up in the Pentecostal church, it always seemed everyone was constantly trying to do their absolute best to be "righteous" and "godly." Now, don't get me wrong; in no way am I criticizing the motives or intentions of these God-fearing people. But, even as a young boy, I couldn't understand why they could never obtain their goal of "righteous living." It seemed almost every week these same people were in the altar repenting for the same things they repented for last week . . . and the week before . . . and the week before! Somehow, I knew there was a missing piece to this puzzle.

One day while in prayer I asked the Lord what the breakdown was in this cycle. Why were these people—me included—always struggling with the same issues over and over and over and over again. Then, I heard the Lord say something that was not only for that moment, but would begin to change my entire thought pattern. He said, *"David, the problem is these people don't know who they are or what I have made them."* As much as I could, I began to wrap my mind and open my spirit to what He had said, but I knew there was much more to that statement than what appeared on the surface. So, I began to pray and search the Scriptures to find exactly what He meant.

Once God began to open my eyes to the Word, it didn't take long to make sense out of what He had spoken to me that day in prayer. The more I studied, the more I could see, while many, many Believers had the right motive and heart to live righteous, they were trying to do so in order to *obtain* a status of righteousness. In other words, in their hearts, the more "right things" they did, the more righteous they would become. Even though this sounds good and "holy," it's not what the Bible says at all! Actually, the Biblical pattern is exactly opposite.

Again, before you throw this book down and shout "heresy," take a look for yourself at what the Bible really says! First, look at what God says about you. Look at what happened to you and how your status changed the very instant you believed on Jesus as your Savior. The Bible says that in that moment, you instantly *became* the righteous of God through Christ. Paul says it this way:

> **"But of Him you are in Christ Jesus, who became for us wisdom from God—and righteousness and sanctification and redemption . . ."**

> **1 Corinthians 1:30**

What an exchange! Jesus, the only person who ever lived on this earth a perfect, sinless, spotless life, took the place of your sin, my sin . . . the sin of the entire world. And what did we get in exchange? Right-standing with God Himself! You traded your *rags* for His *riches*, your *mess* for His *mercy*, and your *garbage* for His amazing, unending *grace*! The Bible clearly says that because of Jesus, and the life you now live in Him, you are righteous . . .

. . . But that's not all.

Paul also encourages Believers in another facet of who they really are when he wrote:

"and be renewed in the spirit of your mind, and that
you put on the new man which was created according
to God, in true righteousness and holiness."

Ephesians 4:23-24

What are Paul's instructions in this verse? Believers should change the way they think (see, I'm not the only one who says that!) and "put on" the very person God has made them to be. We need to stop living as the old man and live as the new man in Christ.

Who is that person? According to this verse, the "new man" has two outstanding characteristics: *righteousness and holiness!* Also, notice that Paul *doesn't* say we all have to "get busy doing what is right so we can earn our stripes of righteousness and holiness." No! There is nothing you or I or anyone else in this world could ever do that would even come close to what Jesus already paid for on the cross of Calvary. This powerful

> *...if you ever really believe what God says you are you will act like it!*

revelation, when received by faith, will totally change the way you see yourself in Christ. Your position changes from "sinner saved by grace" to:

- I AM righteous and

- I AM holy

Now, comes the good part!

SINCE YOU ARE, THEN ACT

I'm a firm believer that if you ever really believe what God says you are you will act like it! While the Law is intended to keep you connected to your old, sinful nature, God's grace frees you to live out who you really are—righteous and holy. The Law renders you powerless, while grace empowers you to be the righteousness of God in Christ and to be holy unto the Lord. The problem that has kept many Christians in bondage is manipulating preachers who want to have some type of spiritual dominance over God's people. They have erroneously taught that the way to *earn* righteousness is to do good deeds and the way to *earn* holiness is to act holy.

But, that is completely backwards!

The Biblical process of living a powerful, fruitful, productive life for the Lord is this:

1.   Know who you are: *righteous* and *holy*

2.   Begin to live like you already are: *righteous* and *holy*

Go back to Paul's revelation of righteousness and holiness in Ephesians chapter four, and you will see this pattern in action. After verse 24 establishes your position of righteousness and holiness, then Paul goes on to describe how you should act:

> *"Therefore, putting away lying . . . for we are members of one another."*
>
> **Ephesians 4:25**

Can you see the Biblical pattern here? Paul says that since you *are* righteous and you *are* holy, then start acting like it! In other words, since you are holy, put on holiness. Since you are righteous, put on righteousness. But how many Christians have the order completely backwards? They struggle to live a "righteous" or "holy" life when all the time, Jesus already has positionally made them what they so earnestly strive to obtain. Now can you see why so many Believers burn out, give up, fall away, and often say, "I just can't live this Christian life!"? And they are absolutely right!

No one can live the righteous or holy life without a revelation of who they are in Christ.

The remainder of Ephesians chapter four is full of Paul's instructions of how righteous and holy people should act. Since you *are* holy, then you shouldn't sin in your anger or give the devil a foothold in your life. (verses 26, 27) Neither should you rob from people (verse 28) nor let corrupt communication come from your mouth, but only speak what is edifying—imparting grace—to those who hear what you say. (verse 29) The Bible goes on to say that since you *are* righteous, then don't grieve the Holy Spirit by having bitterness, wrath, and anger towards anyone (verses 30, 31). Finally, Paul ends this passage by saying to those (you and me.) who are righteous:

"And be kind to one another, tenderhearted, forgiving one another, even as God in Christ forgave you."

Ephesians 4:32

Aren't you glad you are finding out who the "real you" really is? Who you truly are and how God truly sees you? Oh, there's nothing like being free to live the life God's grace has purchased for you to live.

FREE TO BE YOU

Every time I see a commercial on television about identity theft (i.e. credit cards, social security numbers, etcetera) I want to jump up and say, "Hey, I know a plethora of preachers who have stolen the spiritual identities from countless Christians! Can they be charged?"

But, of course, they can't be charged (even though they will face greater judgment).

If you have been a victim of spiritual identity theft, then it's time to rise up and begin to live like who you really are—*the righteousness of God.* The way to start living this new you is to leave behind what you were in Adam and move forward to who you are in Christ! One way to accomplish this feat is to get this revelation rooted inside your spirit: You were created by God to live in righteousness and never created to live in sin. In Adam, sin reigned, but in Christ, righteousness reigns!

You were created by God to live in righteousness and never created to live in sin.

Begin to have a shift concerning the way you speak about and see yourself. Stop giving the devil all the credit for how you used to be and begin talking about your *new* life. Spending more time talking about your old life—what you used to do, the things you were involved in before you met Christ—means you haven't changed residences yet! You are still more connected to what you were in Adam than who you are in Christ. In the same manner, don't be a spiritual schizophrenic—saved one day, not saved the next; on Sundays you are living "in Christ" then on

Monday, it's right back to Adam. Start to know who you are in Christ and only identify with what He has done in your life!

Grace never declares your incompleteness in Adam but only accentuates your completeness in Christ.

Walking in the eternal grace of God is the key to living this new life. And here's good news: Grace never declares your incompleteness in Adam but only accentuates your completeness in Christ. When you start to live as a new creation, remarkable things will happen. You will carry yourself differently, think about yourself and see yourself in an entirely different light. And, maybe for the first time, through God's grace. . .

. . . You will be free to be the real you!

CHAPTER 8

GRACE TO REIGN

I t's easy to see from the Scripture that nothing *you have done* in Adam is more powerful that what *God has done* in Christ! There is no comparison. So, you might be asking yourself, "Well, if that is true, then why do I still struggle with sin? Why don't I act like I'm righteous and holy?" And the answer is quite simple. It all has to do with your focus. When your focus is constantly centered on your lesser and false identity in Adam, guess what? You act like your Adamic nature. In other words, you sin. BUT, when your life is centered around your new, true, higher identity in Christ, guess what? You act just like He has made you—righteous and holy. When you make this shift of focus and attention, you are on your way to living the life Paul describes in Romans chapter five when he said:

". . . much more those who receive abundance of grace and of the gift of righteousness will reign in life through the One, Jesus Christ."

Romans 5:17

Here's another shift for your thinking: You were designed by God to reign in this life! But there is a key to living this victorious life. Did you see it in this verse? It's receiving. Receiving—not trying to gain it by merit—God's abundance of grace and His free gift of righteousness. How do you receive? By believing in your heart. What makes you righteous and your next door neighbor unrighteous? You believed and received and your neighbor didn't. When this revelation is established in your heart and you begin to act on it, watch out! You are about to enter into a life that you might not ever have known even existed. You are about to learn what it truly means to reign in this life.

THE LIFE OF BLESSING, NOT CURSING

I think it's about time for another bold, perhaps shocking, and for some, a controversial shift for your thinking (I guess you have figured out by now that I have a few of those!). Are you ready? Here it is: To every New Testament Christian reading this book, you are *blessed* and not *cursed* . . .

. . . PERIOD!

Ok, now I've stirred up some feathers for sure! And, that's alright. But keep reading and see how living your new life in Christ negates all of your old life—including curses—in Adam. When you reign in life, you have supremacy over the issues in your life *including* demonic activity and curses. Let's see how grace empowers you to do so.

Over the past few years, much attention has been given to the power of curses which can have negative effects and consequences on someone's life. Generational curses, satanic curses, soul curses, etcetera. Again, I'm not denying the fact that these, and many other types of oppressions and satanic attacks exist in the world; however, for the New Testament Believer there is great news:

The New Covenant removes any and all curses!

That's right. If you are a Believer, no one can curse you. No witchdoctor, pastor, leader, friend, or foe. All curses are removed. Now, you might be asking, "What about my bloodline and all the bad things that were handed down to me from past generations?" Well, I have another bit of great news for you: The moment you believed in Jesus and became righteous, *your bloodline changed!* It doesn't matter what kind of scoundrel your father, mother, great-grandfather, or great-great-great-great uncle was . . . YOU ARE A NEW CREATION full of God's abundant, life-changing grace. Now, the question is:

Do you want to keep living under the curses of Adam?
or
Do you want to live under the blessings of your new life?

The choice is yours and seemingly obvious. But, just in case you need some Biblical persuasion, take a look at what God suggests you do:

*"I call heaven and earth as witnesses today against
you, that I have set before you life and death, blessing
and cursing; therefore choose life, that both you and
your descendants may live;"*

Deuteronomy 30:19

Making the choice to live under God's grace and not under the
curse of the past is one of the first steps of learning how to reign
and live victoriously in this life. It's time to forget about your past,
forget your failures, forget about what some distant relative you
never knew has done and live today—right
now—in the grace God has so lavishly poured
out on you. I like to say it this way: Your past
is only fertilizer for your future. Your past is
just a springboard into the life God has for
you now! Focus on the now, so you can taste
the power of the age to come and learn to live
in God's blessings which is His grace towards
you.

*Your past
is only
fertilizer
for your
future.*

And living in His grace is one of the keys
to reigning in this life!

CONSEQUENCES NOT CURSING

Isn't it good to know that under the New Covenant and living under
the cover of grace there are no curses? This might be one of the
greatest revelations for you in this entire book. However, it would
be irresponsible of me to not completely explain that while there
are no *curses* in the New Covenant, there are *consequences* if Biblical
principles are not followed. Allow me to clarify a bit further.

Let's take tithing for an example. Contrary to some popular teaching, not tithing *will not* bring a curse on you under the New Covenant (even though some money-hungry preachers will tell you the opposite). However, there *are* consequences for not honoring God with your financial increase. The truth is: You're not cursed if you don't tithe, but you will be broke! You see, tithing is a principle God set up to appropriate financial blessing to your life. Now, some might say, "Well, isn't tithing under the Law?" and quite honestly the answer is, "No." The principle of tithing came from a man of faith and grace—Abraham—when he met Melchizedek. In that meeting, God made Mankind the absolute best financial deal ever recorded. In essence, God said, "If you will give me ten percent, I will count it as you gave me everything!" I don't know about you, but I think that is the deal of the ages.

> *...while there are no curses in the New Covenant, there are consequences.*

Also, tithing under grace has more to do with your heart than the amount. If you're one of those who give your ten percent—even down to the penny—because you "have to," then you will be the same one who complains, "This tithing stuff just doesn't work." Well, consider what the New Testament says. Second Corinthians 9:7 qualifies that you should give according to the "purposes of your heart, not grudgingly or out of necessity..." When you participate in the principle of tithing, with the right heart, you are blessed. If you don't, you're not cursed, but there are consequences accompanying your lack of action.

Another type of person that religion loves to hang the "cursed" sign on is those who have broken their marriage covenant and participated in adultery. Maybe this is you or someone you know. If so, and you, or they, live under the horrible weight of condemnation, here's another mind shift for you: If a married person falls into the sins of adultery, they are not cursed by God. God will love them, forgive them, and His grace will restore them; however, there can be serious adverse consequences which follow. Their spouse may not be as forgiving. A relationship which took years to build can be dismantled within minutes. Many corporations have now established adultery as grounds for reprimand or dismissal. There's the possibility of divorce with all the financial burdens of two house payments, possible alimony and child support. Not to mention the shock of starting life over again. It's important to realize, God has not cursed the adulterer, but the adulterer will face the cost of their actions.

These are just two examples, but I'm sure you can see the difference. Are people under the New Covenant cursed? Most definitely not. Are there consequences that can arise from not following Biblical principles? Most definitely yes. The best way to live is under the covering of grace, following the principles God has laid out in His Word to bring blessings to your life.

It's how you reign in life!

DEAD, BUT YET ALIVE

Before you can really understand *how* you can actually live this type of life, you must first have a revelation of *what* has qualified you. And, just like receiving God's righteousness, it has absolutely nothing to do with the things you do or don't do. The ability for you to reign in this life is only found one way . . .

. . . Through God's grace!

Take a look at a few verses from Romans chapter six and let's begin to see the fullness of what happened the day Jesus died on the cross.

> *"Or do you not know that as many of us as were baptized into Christ Jesus were baptized into His death? Therefore we were buried with Him through baptism into death, that just as Christ was raised from the dead by the glory of the Father, even so we also should walk in newness of life. For if we have been united together in the likeness of His death, certainly we also shall be in the likeness of His resurrection,"*

Romans 6:3-5

These verses clearly describe the position of every Believer. The Bible says that Jesus not only took our sins to the cross, but that we, as Believers, have been baptized into His death. What this means is that my sin, your sin, and every sin that you have committed or will ever commit was nailed to the cross with our Savior. But, it doesn't stop there. Just as you were planted in the likeness of His death, you were also raised to newness of life in His resurrection. Not only did He carry you to the cross, He raised you—even without your permission!

The fact that you are in Christ makes you a walking dead man. That's right. You live, but your sins have been completely done away with. Now, the question is this: *Do you believe it, and will you identify with it?* Would you rather stay bound to sin and refuse to believe that you really are "in Him" or live in God's grace and be free? Would you rather live under the Law and continue in the lust of the flesh or live righteously (because you are righteous) under the covering of grace? If you are struggling with the two—sin and grace—consider this truth: God's grace will never, ever keep you bound to sin, but rather it causes you to know that you are free!

The first step to freedom is agreeing with what Christ did on the cross. It really is that simple: just believe. If reigning in life by believing and living under God's grace is so easy, then why do so many Christians struggle with sin issues? I believe the answer to this question is this: They spend too much time visiting the graveyard where their old sinful nature is buried!

God's grace will never, ever keep you bound to sin, but rather it causes you to know that you are free!

And they try to bring it back to life.

DO NOT RESUSCITATE

Far too many Believers live between two identities—one in Christ, the other in Adam. They constantly jump the fence back and forth. One day in Christ, the next day back in Adam. One day "blessed," the next day "cursed." Even though this seems like a major spiritual hindrance, what it really boils down to is a lack of spiritual maturity.

Understand that spiritual maturity many times does not relate to how long someone has been born again and serving God. There are those who have been in the faith for 40, 50, and even 60 years, but have lived more connected to Adam than Christ, thus they have never grown past the basics of "I'm saved and on my way to Heaven." Now, in no way do I undermine the glory of having an eternal life with Jesus; however, there is more to being a Christian than escaping hell.

It is the grace to reign in *this life*, right now!

One thing that will always try to sway you back to the old Adamic nature and steal your new life experience is something the Bible calls your "old man" (See Ephesians 4:22 and Colossians 3:9), or in easier terms, the old manner of life you used to live. For most of us, that old nature came back to visit not too soon after we had believed on Jesus and changed residences! But, remember what we just read? Jesus took that sin to the cross, including your old way of life. Now, look how Paul continues to describe how the cross affects our lives:

> *"Knowing this, that our old man was crucified with Him, that the body of sin might be done away with, that we should no longer be slaves of sin."*

> **Romans 6:6**

Notice something interesting about this scripture that differs from the previous ones we just read. In verses three through five, Paul says that two things happen to those who are in Christ: They are buried AND are resurrected to a new life with Him. Now, look at how your old man is different. That old nature was crucified with Christ, BUT there is no sign of life. As a matter of fact, the Scripture says it was completely done away with. I love the way the Message Bible translates this verse. It says:

> *"Could it be any clearer? Our old way of life was nailed to the cross with Christ, a decisive end to*

> *that sin-miserable life—no longer at sin's every beck and call!"*
>
> **Romans 6:6 (MSG)**

What happened to your old man? That joker was crucified—nailed to cross! What once controlled and dominated your life is now done away with, discarded, defeated, and dead. So, since your old, corrupt nature is dead, why give it CPR? Why resurrect it? Why jump the fence and go back to the graveyard, where your old Adamic nature is lying in death, and dig it up? You're not called to go back and live there. You are dead to the old man, dead to sin, and now have a brand new life powered by God's supernatural grace!

I am convinced that when you come to the realization that you are dead to sin, you will stop living in sin. The more you focus on your new life in Christ—the reigning life by God's amazing grace—the more power you will experience over the temptation of sin. Will there always be temptation? Yes. But, the more you identify with the resurrection of Christ, the more you will see the true condition of your old man—dead! God's grace and His gift of righteousness revealed in you will keep you out of the graveyard, place you on the right side of the fence, and position you to reign in life. Now, your job is to believe it and appropriate what Jesus finished on the cross into your own life. How do you do this? It starts by changing your confession and doing what the Bible says holy and righteous people do: avoid corrupt communication.

...when you come to the realization that you are dead to sin, you will stop living in sin.

THE GREATEST HINDERENCE

Over the years of teaching thousands of people how to live in the grace of God and subsequently reign in this life, I would dare say that the number one enemy which limits Believers from fully living in God's abundant life is *not* the devil—even though he gets credited most of the time. No, what normally keeps Christians from experiencing all God has is what comes out of their own mouths! Remember what Paul said in Ephesians 4:29? In this verse, he's saying that since you are righteous and holy, then this is one thing that should accompany you:

> *"Let no corrupt word proceed out of your mouth, but what is good for necessary edification, that it may impart grace to the hearers."*

Undoubtedly, most Christians only think of one thing when they read this scripture: "I shouldn't curse!" And while that's probably a good standard to live by, "corrupt communication" in this context of this scripture is not talking about four-lettered words at all. What it is referring to is the Law coming out of your mouth! That's far more corrupt than cursing. When you speak about yourself in any fashion other than how Jesus, through God's grace, sees you, it is corrupt communication. In other words, Paul is saying, "Since you are holy, don't talk about yourself or others as under the Law; only speak what grace says."

And Paul wasn't the first to recognize the power of this principle.

In the Old Testament (again, before the age of grace), there was a man named Isaiah. One day, God granted him an open vision where Isaiah saw into the supernatural realm. Look how the Bible beautifully describes this encounter:

> *"In the year that King Uzziah died, I saw the Lord sitting on a throne, high and lifted up, and the train of His robe filled the temple. Above it stood seraphim; each one had six wings: with two he covered his face, with two he covered his feet, and with two he flew."*

Isaiah 6:1-2

Can you only imagine this experience? Actually seeing the Lord, high and lifted up and all of His glory filling the temple! What would it be like to bask in the radiance and holiness of God filling every single cell surrounding you? Isaiah was there; completely surrounded by the presence of Almighty God. Then, the frailty of his flesh was immediately brought to light as he said:

> *"Woe is me, for I am undone! Because I am a man of unclean lips, and I dwell in the midst of a people of unclean lips; for my eyes have seen the King, the Lord of hosts."*

Isaiah 6:5

Notice something extremely important about this verse. What was the only thing Isaiah described as "unclean?" Not his hands or his feet or his eyes. No, there was only one thing that fit into this category—his mouth! How interesting to compare Isaiah's revelation of his mouth being something "unclean" and the Apostle Paul listing "corrupt communication" as something holy people do not participate in. However, Isaiah did not remain "unclean," as the Bible says an angel took a live burning coal from the altar, touched his mouth, and said:

> *". . . Behold, this has touched your lips; your iniquity is taken away, and your sin purged."*

> **Isaiah 6:7**

At some point in our lives, we all need this purging. Sometimes, more than once! Thank God that it's not by a live burning coal from the altar of God delivered by an angel. Today, this purging of the tongue and what comes out of our mouths is done by the grace of God. It's a transformation of the mind and heart which allows us to see and speak of ourselves from our position of righteousness and holiness—not our defeated, sinful nature. Now, by the power of grace, "I'm unclean" changes to "I'm righteous and holy!"

Now, let's bring it down to where you live. Do you want to stop the corrupt communication from proceeding out of your mouth, thus keeping you from reigning in life through God's grace? Sure you do. So, here's a challenge, somewhere to start and build from. Now that you have the revelation of how your old, sinful nature was crucified with Christ at the cross, I want you to stop saying "I need to stop sinning." You see, that statement focuses on sin—the Law. Instead, shift your focus, and from your position of righteousness, begin to say:

> **"Since sin is dead in me, I no longer have to participate!"**

Now, your focus is on the sustaining grace of God that gives you the ability to rise above sin. This is the beginning of how you reign in this life through grace! What proceeds out of your mouth is so powerful and can keep you bound to sin or free in righteousness and grace. Thank God that Jesus took your sin, nailed it to the cross, and rendered it helpless forever. Now, it's time to start thinking, speaking, and acting like it's true. It's time to live this abundant life Jesus has already paved the way for you to enjoy!

REIGN IN THIS LIFE

You are resurrected with Christ in a new life. Your old manner of life is dead and buried. Corrupt communication is ceasing to proceed out of your mouth. You are well on your way to living your new life—reigning with Christ! Now, here is one more element that will help you continue further on your journey:

> *"Likewise you also, reckon yourselves to be dead indeed to sin, but alive to God in Christ Jesus our Lord. Therefore do not let sin reign in your mortal body, that you should obey it in its lusts."*

> **Romans 6:11-12**

Remember, the only way your old man is ever coming back to life is if you resuscitate it! Since the old man is dead, why don't you just agree with it and act like it's dead? This is the same principle we saw with being righteous and holy. Since you are righteous, act righteous. In the same light, since your old man is dead, act like it. Live like you're free. Live resurrected with Jesus. With the understanding of this powerful revelation, I contend that, under the New Covenant, no Christian has the right to just keep doing wrong simply because they just "can't help themselves." That's an excuse of the flesh! Someone who thinks they cannot stop sinning is actually confessing that they have no idea what or who they are in Christ. Think about it. Do you think someone who loves the Lord really wants to continue struggling with sin issues? Of course not. But, as long as they never know they are free, their fight and frustration will continue.

You see, just because you don't walk in your new life doesn't mean you don't have it! The choice is yours. My question is: Why would you want to live a life lesser than what you are called to? Why would you live like a pauper while being a king? I didn't say you would be perfect, but even if you have blown it, GET UP! Jesus never came to this earth to condemn sin, but *He never applauded it either*. Whatever has disqualified you in Adam, Christ has redeemed and qualified you to partake in His resurrection and life.

It's time to take your rightful place and begin to reign in this life through One, Christ Jesus. Sin is not the root issue—even though religious teachers of the Law would like you to think so! The issues are: Knowing who you are in Christ, realizing your sin is dead and never going back to revive it, and living like you are resurrected with Him. Again, this is the foundation Paul talked about of how to reign in this life.

You cannot live in grace without knowing that Christ died for your sins, and you cannot mention His death without declaring that no matter how much sin is abounding, grace does so much more abound! In other words, the darker it gets, the brighter your light shines. A floodlight does no good in broad daylight, but in the darkness, it completely illuminates everything in its path. And that spiritual floodlight is someone—you and I—who walk in God's grace. It's someone—you and I—who know how to live above sin.

It's someone—you and I—who know, by God's grace how to reign in this life!

CHAPTER 9

GRACE IN A NEW LIGHT

As you have journeyed through the pages of this book, it is my prayer that somewhere along the way, perhaps in many areas, God has begun to reveal the truth of His amazing grace. Believe me; the more you learn about grace, the more you really see how much you didn't know or how wrong you were previously taught. My life is a testimony to this fact, as I have been studying and teaching on grace principles for years, and it never ceases to amaze me just how much there is still to learn. The Word of God is a living, breathing organism which continues to produce life and revelation to anyone who will open their heart, pray, and ask God to continually reveal His Word. For me, and hopefully for you, it's the journey of a lifetime!

While there has been much information and revelation brought forth in this book, I wanted to take a chapter to reinforce some principles and thoughts in a bit more palatable format. To do so,

I would like to use some different acronyms using these letters G.R.A.C.E. Now, if you have been around church-life for any length of time, you will have undoubtedly heard of the most classic definition of grace as God's Riches At Christ's Expense. And while this is a wonderful and beautiful description, I believe we have seen how the life of grace is much more encompassing.

We have briefly covered a few of the areas in different sections and chapters, but I believe seeing it in this light will enhance what you have seen, expound on what you have already learned, and help you to grow in your understanding of God's incredible gift to us all—His amazing grace. I trust you will enjoy this fresh look as we see the power of G.R.A.C.E. in a new light.

GOD'S REDEMPTIVE AFFIRMATION
CAPTURING EVERYONE

Have you ever stopped for a moment and just meditated on the awesomeness of redemption? Several times in this book, we have talked about the power of redemption and how Jesus "bought us back" to God through His blood, but it is—and will be—the foundation of everything we live and enjoy in the Kingdom of God. Of all the revelation and spiritual insight you will ever receive from walking with the Lord, this one aspect of grace should continually blow your mind. I can speak from experience that just taking some time to stop and think about what God did, through Jesus at the cross, can calm practically any emotional storm and put everything back into perspective.

Oh, thank God for His redemption and grace!

Even though God's master plan of redemption is something we may never fully comprehend, it needs a few components at work for someone to get saved. Actually, when someone believes on the Lord Jesus and becomes born again, there are three distinct factors—much like a spiritual Tri-fecta—at work. Look how the Apostle Paul explains these three elements working together:

"For by grace you have been saved through faith, and that not of yourselves; it is the gift of God,"

Ephesians 2:8

Can you see how this scripture displays the new birth experience as a beautiful blend of grace, faith, and belief? Jesus, by virtue of His death, burial, and resurrection, released the grace of God upon the earth, and that grace was the ticket for anyone to enter the Kingdom of God. But, there had to be some action taken in order for this grace to be applied. Salvation was made available at the cross but never becomes a reality *until* the day someone activates faith and (here's this word again) *believes!* And, where do you get the faith to believe? It is a wonderful "gift from God." So, in the working of redemption, here is a breakdown of what happens:

1. Jesus paved the way of grace at the cross.

2. God provided the gift of faith.

3. We believed and were saved!

The redemptive plan of God has been fully executed. Faith is available for any and everyone to call on the name of the Lord. BUT, if you never have believed, then here's the reality: You're not saved. Just two of the three elements (grace and faith) aren't enough! You must believe in your heart and receive God's free gift of righteousness and redemption. If you have never taken that step and believed on Jesus, let me assure of something that might surprise you: *God's not mad at you!* Think about it. Why would He be mad? He's already done everything He is ever going to do to secure your eternal redemption. His grace is overflowing to you. His grace is abounding to you. It's been extended to you.

> *God's grace is only bestowed upon those who believe.*

But, here's a truth that every unbeliever needs to realize:

God's grace is only bestowed upon those who believe.

Let me encourage you, if you have never taken the time to believe on the Lord Jesus and accept the life-changing grace of God, why not now? Maybe you have read this book and for the first time have seen the truth that God is not mad at you or punishing you for all the "wrong" you have done. Believe me, no matter how many times you hear the "you better get saved or you'll burn in hell" message, if that is your only reason for coming to Jesus, you will probably only settle for the spiritual "fire insurance" and never experience the fullness of God's grace in action!

Redemption is paid for and is free for the taking. Grace is in full measure to meet you where you are. God has provided the gift of faith. Now, take that step—that one step which requires action from you . . . and believe. Become a part of God's family and become a recipient of His grace: His redemptive affirmation capturing everyone . . .

. . . Including you!

GOD REMOVING ALL CONDEMNING ELEMENTS

I would dare say that 9 out of 10 people who have ever learned a Bible verse probably learned John 3:16 first. Whether it was from Sunday School, Vacation Bible School, or on their grandma's knee, they learned that God loved our world so much that He sent Jesus, and everyone who believed on Him would live forever in Heaven. Even though I love this verse and the incredible hope it brings to a lost world, I've always wondered why the very next verse was seemingly always overlooked, even though it's in the same context of Scripture. As a matter of fact, I know Christians who have been in church and serving the Lord for years who STILL have no idea what that verse says! To me, they flow hand-in-hand, and one is the continuation of the other. So, why don't we look at that next verse:

> *"For God did not send His Son into the world to condemn the world, but that the world through Him might be saved."*
>
> **John 3:17**

When you see these two verses together, it's very obvious that not only did Jesus come to this earth to *do* something; He also came *not to do* something else. What He came *to do* was save the world from their sins. Just as importantly, what He *didn't come to do* was condemn the world of all the wrong they had done. (As a side note,

I think the reason Jesus didn't have to condemn the world is because Christians have done a good enough job of it on our own . . . without His help!)

Two of the most diabolical terms you will ever encounter are the words "grace" and "condemnation." Grace is the agent that brings you into the Kingdom of God; condemnation is the evil that keeps you connected to your past life full of mistakes. Grace brings a covering of God's love and mercy; condemnation keeps your future tied to your past. Condemnation, along with its cohort, guilt, will always scream, "You should be ashamed;" while grace, on the other hand, mercifully says, "If you've done nothing wrong or if you've done everything wrong, you should never be ashamed!"

> *"If you've done nothing wrong or if you've done everything wrong, you should never be ashamed!"*

Here's another Biblical truth that will help differentiate between the worlds of grace and condemnation: While grace removes the greatest weapon of satan and religion: *condemnation,* it also released the greatest tool of the Spirit: *conviction.* The two (condemnation and conviction) are not the same. Consider these points:

- Conviction is God dealing with areas in your life . . . in love . . . which need to change. Condemnation is activated through guilt and religious mindsets designed to weigh you down.

- Conviction produces repentance and hope. Condemnation produces shame and a feeling of uselessness.

- Conviction empowers and qualifies you. Condemnation robs your peace and seeks to disqualify.

In 1423, the great reformer, Martin Luther, declared these powerful words:

"God doesn't seek to damn, but to regenerate mankind and give him a new chance at life."

Wow, that sounds a whole lot like John chapter three verses 16 AND 17 doesn't it? More than just a feel-good statement, this is really grace at work! Now, let's take it a step further. The issue is settled through the Word that God is a God of grace, but the big question is: How do we—His Body on this earth—represent this grace? Do we walk in that same grace and acceptance towards others? Or do we live a life full of condemnation and disapproval?

I think the honest answers might scare us!

It never, ever ceases to amaze me how the Church is the only living entity that enjoys killing their own! It's really nothing less than the spirit of murder loosed in the Body of Christ. Not physical murder with guns and knives, but emotional and spiritual murder drawn from a much more powerful weapon: our mouths. I'm more convinced that if it wasn't for weather and the latest high-profile Christian leader to fall into sin, most Believers wouldn't have much to talk about! My question is: Where is grace? Where is the God of the second chance that we all preach about?

Sadly, it often seems easier to preach it than live it.

Friend, we must understand that if, in our pursuit of grace, we become Holy Ghost prosecutors—judging everyone else who is not just like us as "invalid"—then we are no freer than the people we condemn. The Bible says we are "ambassadors," not "judges." (2 Corinthians 5:20) The problem is that while you walk around all day and say, "I'm not a legalist; I'm under grace," and yet, at the same time, point out every spec of legalism in someone else's life, then there is no difference between them and you! You've only traded one set of legalism for another form of self-righteousness.

Maybe you've thrown the book at someone who committed adultery because they "broke the commandment." Well, before you do, remember it was Jesus, under the New Covenant, who said that if you just looked at someone with lust in your heart, you're just as guilty! (Matthew 5:28) Also, take into account how Jesus responded the day He came face-to-face with someone caught red-handed in the act of adultery. Religion said, "Stone her. She has broken the Law," but after putting all of the religious hypocrites in their place, what did Jesus say? "I'm not here to condemn you. Get up, go on your way, and stop living this way." (John 8:11) And that's exactly what she did.

Let's face it. Everybody has issues they are constantly dealing with. *Everybody!* No one is without problems and scrutiny, but when you focus on grace, your attention shifts from a person's failures to the God of restoration! Religion will always try to take the whip of legalism and beat the life out of people. But here's some great news:

Jesus showed up and took the whip away!

John 1:14 portrays two of the most beautiful qualities of Jesus. In this verse, the Bible describes Jesus as the One who was "full of grace and truth." If these were two of Jesus' distinct attributes while on the earth, doesn't it make sense that we—His bodily representation on the earth today—should carry and be full of the same things? Sadly, too many of His representatives (a.k.a. Christians) have exchanged "grace and truth" for "judgment and condemnation." Even sadder is the effect this has had on the mission of Christianity throughout the world. Never has this been so evident than in the words of Mahatma Gandhi as he once said:

> ***"If Christians would really live according to the teachings of Christ, as found in the Bible, all of India would be Christian today."***

Obviously, there has been some breakdown in the way Christians present their Christ as India has been the birth place of four major religions: Hinduism, Jainism, Buddhism, and Sikhism. A 2001 census also reported that India is 80% Hindu, 15% Muslim, and only 1.3% Christian. We can only speculate how this great nation would have been radically different if, in fact, Christians would have been a true representative of their Savior—full of grace and truth.

Not only does the advancement of the global Kingdom of God suffer when Christians do not act like their Christ, but it is also detrimental to one's personal spiritual growth. I am convinced that these two elements—grace and truth—are not just two words randomly connected together in the description of Jesus. They are spiritual characteristics and principles that work hand-in-hand together. I also believe it to be true that, for any Believer, the amount of grace you show directly determines the amount of truth you walk in. Do you want more truth? Then walk in more grace! Do you pray for more revelation of God's Word? Your answer lies in the amount of God's grace you display!

Oh, for grace to know Him more.

There's nothing as fulfilling as being an instrument of God's grace on the earth. In becoming His true ambassador, here's something to always remember: Grace is not conditional or compartmentalized. Jesus came to remove ALL condemnation and guilt, not just part of it. So, while it's wonderful to have grace and compassion on the Muslim, Buddhist, Hindu, or terrorist who basically hate Christianity, don't forget to activate that same grace towards another blood-bought Believer. Sure, they might see the Scriptures in a little different light than you, but they are part of your Kingdom family. In the same manner, if you can have compassion for someone on the other side of the world, be sure to cut the guy who comes to church with tattoos and earrings some slack! Learn to walk in grace for all, especially the ones you don't agree with.

> *The amount of grace you show directly determines the amount of truth you walk in.*

While you are living and sharing God's grace with others, please don't forget to include the person who might need it the most: *yourself!* Finding grace for yourself is usually never easy. In most cases, the number one reason for this dilemma is because you know yourself better than anyone else alive! You know your faults, weaknesses, failures, temptations, and flaws. Never forget that in your weakness, HE is made strong (2 Corinthians 12:9); and even with your flaws, in Christ, you are flawless. Always bestow the same grace to yourself as you do to others. You will be glad you did.

People may never extend to you the grace that you have extended to them. That's okay; give them grace anyway. If you are going to err, at least err on the side of loving too much and showing too much grace. Choose to focus on God's eternal grace not only for your salvation, but for others—and most importantly, for yourself! Be Christ's real representative—full of grace of truth—and show the world that God, through His abundant grace, truly did remove all the condemning elements!

GOD'S RIGHTEOUSNESS AND CORRESPONDING ENABLEMENT

While we have already spent a fair bit of time on the subject of righteousness, I want to take this particular section and expound on not only what it is, but also what it does. It will also not hurt to reinstate some truths and strengthen some principles we have already seen in an earlier chapter.

First, let me reiterate that no one has or will ever become righteous simply by what they do. If you simply try to please God by the good things you *do* or the bad things you *don't* do, those qualifications alone will not equal nor provide you a righteous state of being. Righteousness is a position afforded to you totally on what Jesus did and provided at the cross. In saying this, let me also bring home a point that somehow seems to be overlooked, misconstrued, or completely abandoned in the message of grace. It is this: For one to walk and live in righteousness and grace, repentance is mandatory. It is vitally important to know that:

Repentance leads one to grace, and grace leads one to repentance.

Too many times, people want to divide grace and repentance; but in reality, they are directly related to each other. Actually, you can't have one without the other! Grace without repentance leads to universalism. Repentance without grace leads to legalism. Grace and repentance together lead to salvation.

Grace is not just what saves you; it is also what empowers you.

But the journey doesn't stop at repentance. Honestly, that is just the very beginning of a new life in Christ. A new life of God's grace. It's so unfortunate that many, many Christians never get past the one aspect of salvation. By grace are they saved, but the remainder of their Christian life is more of a rollercoaster ride to Heaven than the abundant life Jesus promised they could enjoy on this earth. (John 10:10) I believe one of the most important aspects of God's grace that any Christian can grab ahold of is this: Grace is not just what saves you; it is also what empowers you.

When someone is empowered, it simply means they have been given authority to act. Many people who are up in years give someone close to them power of attorney which authorizes that person to make legal decisions on their behalf. Empowerment is authority. This is exactly grace in action: Your Kingdom authority, through your position of righteousness, which grants you the ability to live holy unto to the Lord! As I said before, and it bears repeating, grace takes away the "want to" to live an unholy life.

Over the course of this book, my stand against legalists and religious-minded people has been made very clear. However, I must say there is one thing that will kill a person's spirit and walk with God even quicker than legalism and religion. It is the demonic mindset that grace is nothing more than a "license to sin and get away with it." Nothing could be further from the truth. On the contrary, a life empowered by God's grace says, "I want to live right. I want to give more. I want more accountability. I want to do everything I can to please my God!"

This only comes from an empowerment of grace.

When my four sons each reached the age to get their driver's license, I remember sitting each of them down and saying something like this. "Son, the piece of laminated paper in your wallet is powerful. It allows you to operate a vehicle that is intended to be a blessing, but if not operated properly, it can also become an instrument of destruction. You can, right now, take your car and start driving down the wrong side of the interstate— your license will allow you to do so. But I would have to tell you . . . that probably would not be the smartest move because judgment would soon come in the fact that you would hit someone head-on. You can do it if you choose, but it's not the best, most profitable choice."

The license says, "You can drive," but acting in complete lawlessness would have produced death.

The same exact spiritual principle applies to living the life of grace. The Apostle Paul puts it best when he says that, under the covering of grace, everything is lawful but not everything is beneficial. Or, in other words, not everything is in your best interest. (1 Corinthians 10:23) Just because you are free from the Law doesn't release you from the obligations and responsibilities which are still principles. I like to say it like this:

> ***Jesus came to redeem us from the curse, but not remove our awareness of it.***

Think of it like this. The Law was the schoolmaster which brought you to a governor (grace). If you completely forget the schoolmaster, you will then abandon the governor. In other words, if you forget how you got to this place of righteousness, then you will forget what brought you here!

You might be wondering what all of this has to do with righteousness and its enabling power. Everything! I would never intend for anyone to have any inclination that righteousness and grace are just haphazard, easy-go-lucky, spiritual certifications to do whatever you want, when you want. The Apostle Paul addressed this exact same thought and had the right response:

> **"What then? Shall we sin, because we are not under the law, but under grace? God forbid."**
>
> **Romans 6:15 (KJV)**

And the answer is still the same today—God forbid!

The good news is: You can be aware of the Law but do not have to live a life under the Law. You can be aware of sin, but live your life above sin. It is true that you can really be in this world but not of it. And there's only one way to accomplish this life—to live empowered by God's grace: His righteousness and corresponding enablement.

GOD RADICALLY ACCEPTING CREATION ETERNALLY

Ask a room full of religious-minded Christians if they believe in the power of redemption, and they all will unanimously respond, "Yes, amen! Thank God for redemption." Well, that's fairly easy to comprehend since, at one time in their lives, they were lost without Christ and now have believed on Jesus and accepted His redemptive work on the cross for their sins. Now, ask that same group if they believe that this redemptive power is available for everyone—the practicing homosexual, the murderer, the rapist, the pedophile, the unfaithful husband/wife—and you might not get such a resounding, "Amen." In fact, you will probably get more grunts than approval.

Religious-minded people—*those who are more interested in exposing what you were in Adam rather than revealing what you are in Christ*—have always hoarded the power of redemption as a "us four and no more" mentality. For them, it's much easier to rationalize how God can save those who really "weren't all that bad," but it's a stretch to see how God could pardon someone who is a "rank sinner." This type of thinking is usually based out of fear and has nothing to do with faith. Meaning, those who succumb to this thought (that redemption may not be for everyone) are scared to death to even talk to the practicing homosexual who rides their bus to work or the prostitute down the street! They are so intimidated, and most times, disgusted by their "sin" that they never even try to reach out with the love and grace of God.

They are just "too bad" for God to love.

Well, then the question would have to be answered: "Who sets the standard of what is 'too bad' for redemption?" And the answer is simple: *There is no such meter.* The reality is all of us—every person who has ever walked on this planet—is lost until they believe, by faith, on the Lord Jesus. When Jesus shed His blood on the cross and released the grace of God into the earth, there was no distinction line drawn for those who are "real bad" and those who are "not so bad." We were all lost and without God.

Go back to the scripture we referenced earlier: *"For God so loved the world . . ."* (John 3:16) When the Bible says, *". . . the world,"* it means exactly that—everyone who has or who will ever live on this planet. From the person who has never done anything "wrong" to the person who is given to a reprobate mind—God sent His Son, Jesus, for us all!

I've said it before, and I will keep on saying it until I go to Heaven: No one can ever be "too bad" that they cannot qualify for redemption; neither can anyone be "too good" where they are excluded from redemption. Adam blew it for all, but Jesus came to redeem all—the good, the not-so-good, and the flat-out mean and ugly! It is His grace in action—His radical acceptance of creation eternally.

WALK IN THE LIGHT

Maybe this chapter has helped you to see G.R.A.C.E. in a totally different light. If so, let me encourage you to start living in the light which has been given to you. The Bible says to "walk in the light as He (Jesus) is in the light." (1 John 1:7) Remember, revelation is progressive and as long as you live, God's Word—which includes His grace—should always be developing in your heart.

Let's now take the wonderful message of God's grace to the world as we live and walk in our divine calling . . .

. . . Empowered by His amazing, supernatural grace!

CHAPTER 10

GRACE IN THE SECOND DIMENSION

Ralph Waldo Emerson once said, "Life is a journey, not a destination," and the longer you live, the more you realize the truth of this statement. Of course, no one could have convinced my sons of this fact when they were younger and always asking the all-so-familiar Huskins family road trip question, "Dad, are we there yet?" or "Dad, how much longer before we get there?" Which my answer was inevitably, "We're about 10 minutes closer from the last time you asked!" Too bad they were too young to really enjoy the journey.

As my sons grew older, each one of them came to the day every teenager has circled on their mental calendar—high school graduation! I remember watching many of their friends look at that day as the end-all-be-all—like it was the grand prize of life—

but I planted a different seed into my sons. I remember telling them something like, "Son, I am so proud of you and all you have accomplished in high school. Your graduation is one of the biggest days of your life, but you must realize that this is just the beginning, not the end. The reason they call it a 'commencement' service is because it's the start of a brand new life." It didn't take long after graduation for them to realize how true that statement really was.

The wonderful journey of life is multi-facet and expands beyond what you accomplish and do in the natural. It also encompasses your spiritual growth and walk as well. For example, many new Believers (much like my young sons on road trips), are more focused on the destination than the journey. The minute they gave their life to Jesus and experienced salvation, it's like something inside of them said, "Mission accomplished!" They obtained their ultimate spiritual prize. Even though salvation is a wonderful gift from God, in actuality, it's much like graduation—a commencement or a beginning of a brand new life. Jesus Himself called it the "abundant life" and abundant it is . . .

. . . Full of God's grace.

NOT SAVED "FROM" BUT "FOR"

We have already established the fact that God's grace was one of the elements at work the day you were saved, but that was just the beginning. There is an entirely different function of grace which goes far beyond salvation. I know we love to sing how God's amazing grace "saved a wretch like me," but if you stop there, it's like never living one day after high school graduation. Salvation is a spiritual commencement ceremony! Not only did God have grace to save you, but He also has unlimited grace available to live this abundant life.

This second part of grace, which goes beyond salvation, is the grace you use on a regular basis. I like to call it: grace for your race. In other words, it is the ability to accomplish what God has called and gifted you to do. A simple way to understand the differences between grace that saves and grace that empowers is: Saving grace carried you, but you carry empowering grace. Saving grace was done *in* you while empowering grace is what's *on* you.

> *...saving grace carried you, but you carry empowering grace.*

The problem with most Christians today is they never get past the fact that they have been saved "from something." If this is you, thank God you're saved and on your way to Heaven and not hell; but let me tell you, there is so much more to this walk of faith. Not only has grace saved you "*from* something," but just as importantly, God has also saved you "*for* something." And what is that "something" you are saved for?

Your holy, sovereign, calling that you *and only you* can fulfill in this life!

When Believers only know what they have been saved "from" and not what they have been saved "for," they spend the majority of their Christian life battling the same old habits and lifestyles. They live on a spiritual rollercoaster all the way to Heaven. For example, if someone has been saved from a life of drugs and sexual immorality, quite possibly those weaknesses will always be a struggle, *if* they only have the knowledge of what grace saved them *from*. While they might wholeheartedly embrace the grace which carried them to salvation, it's only a fraction of what God has available.

Saving grace delivers you *from* something, but empowering grace delivers you *for* something: your purpose, call, and God-given assignment here on this earth. What you came out from is gone and was done away with at the cross. You're redeemed from the past! However, if you are constantly using your past mistakes, sins, and failures to run from the purposes of God, then your past is more prevalent to you than your future! Maybe you've said things like, "I've been divorced. God can never use me," or "Since I've spent time in jail, I can only be used by God on a limited basis." These are just a pack of lies from the enemy, and the awesome truth of the Good News is:

While the first grace removed your past, the second grace gives you the ability to pick up and move forward to what God has in store for you!

You are redeemed from the curse of the Law along with all of its fear and intimidations. That was the act of saving grace. Now, any Law, attitude, or motive which tries to drag you back and make you feel less than what God says about you is eradicated by this second dimension of grace! Why? Because living under God's empowering grace gives you the boldness to declare, "I am absolutely authorized and equipped to accomplish everything I was saved *for*."

If you only stop at the first grace and refuse to move into the second grace, then you've missed the whole heart of the Gospel. And who knows, what you thought was going to kill you might be the very thing that qualifies you for the next thing God has for you to do! Who's to say that all your mess wasn't a divine set up for you to bring life to those who are going through those same situations right now? The first step is to change your focus and stop always running *from* sin and begin to run headlong into all God has in store *for* you. When you do, watch out! It won't be long before you start to realize that you are empowered by God to do something spectacular for His Kingdom!

The true testimony of grace is not what God delivered you *from*, but what God has delivered you *for*.

GRACE TO LIVE

Beginning to understand the second dimension of grace and how it works in your everyday life is almost like being born again . . . again. Not only does it bring the revelation of God's overall plan and purpose for your life, it also provides the strength and fortitude to live out that plan on an everyday basis. And trying to live out the plan of God without his grace is like trying to run a race car with no oil. Some type of breakdown is inevitable!

We all know people who occupy positions and do certain things in life that seem to be way out of our realm of comprehension. Not that we couldn't do some of these same things, but not without a trail of wounded people and emotional shrapnel scattered all over the place! So, how do certain people put up with things in life and carry themselves in a certain way? The answer is simple: they're graced for it. Why is it that some people seem to handle every adversity without completely falling apart? Again, they're graced for it. I've even seen some children who have a grace on their life, and everything they live, do, and breathe is aimed at a particular direction and laced with a specific cause.

It's God second dimension of grace at work.

Even though I love to teach people and have a grace to do so, I still look at school teachers and think to myself, "My Lord, how do they do what they do every day—day in and day out—without loosing their minds?" (Especially junior high teachers!) The answer? The ones who don't lose their minds and love what they do are graced to do it. It's the same in every arena of life. Those who effectively pastor people have a grace to accomplish their mission. But grace is not limited to those who are in the five-fold ministry. It is also extended to those in the fields of education, medicine, drama and art, business, the legal world, and many, many others. Anywhere someone is doing something exceptionally creative in the area God has called them to, you can be guaranteed it's a display of God's grace at work!

So many people—good, church-going, tithing, God-fearing people—get saved and spend the rest of their lives sitting on the bench. For the next 35, 40, even 50 years, they occupy space on this earth, die, and go to Heaven but never do one thing God has graced them to do. Why? Because they never learn to live past God's saving grace. It's true for any Believer: If you never live in the second dimension of grace, you will never accomplish everything God has assigned you to do. The good news is you can move to the next level of grace and live your life like God has designed and complete every task He has set in place for you. But you can only accomplish this in one way:

Through God's empowering grace!

WALK IT OUT

Living the life surrounded, engaged, and promoted through the marvelous grace of God is a life like none other. Not only will you find spiritual, emotional, and physical strength to carry out daily tasks, which lead to the completion of a greater work, but this life provides something very hard to find outside of grace: *the incredible sense of fulfillment.* I have come to find out that no matter how much money one has, it is no match for a life that is in pursuit of a purpose, fueled by grace, and fulfilled by its accomplishments. In other words, there is no better life than living right in the middle of what God has called you to do, created you to perform, and graced you to finish the task.

It's the abundant life!

Even while enjoying all of God's blessings and grace, don't be blinded by the fact that every day is a rose garden or is peachy. Oh no, there are many times of struggle, disappointment, discouragement, and sometimes the flat-out temptation to quit! Grace is what keeps your eyes on the prize and finds a way to keep you going when everything and everyone around says to give up. Oh, to know, understand, and live in that grace.

Because I am so passionate about the importance of teaching and expounding on grace's second dimension, I want to take a few minutes and give some very practical points which I believe will benefit and encourage you in your journey. In doing so, I want to use a story found in Genesis chapter four which most people— Believers and non-believers alike—will be familiar with. Even though you may recognize the passage, it might have a few extra nuggets to help you navigate through your walk of grace.

Genesis chapter four is the story of the first sons born to Adam and Eve named Cain and Abel. Now, when most people hear of these two men, the first thing that comes to their mind is murder, and sadly, this story does record the first act of violence in the Bible. Even sadder is this act was taken out one brother against another. However, more than just a story of envy and hatred, this passage teaches some powerful, key principles of walking in all God has graced you to do. Let's take a look at some practical and helpful ways to keep you living in the second dimension of God's grace.

EMBRACE THE PROCESS

I, more than anyone I know, love the fact that we live in a world of instant access, instant production, and instant results. Back in the fifties, fast food restaurants introduced us to an instant world by offering drive-thru windows. Who ever heard of driving to a window, placing your order—never leaving your car—and rolling out with your burger and fries? But the drive-thru was only the beginning. Microwave ovens soon followed which could cook your entire meal at home in less time than it took to warm the oven! Fast forward a few more years to today where we can have instantaneous access to our money through ATM's and connect instantly with practically anyone in world through the Internet. Undoubtedly, our society has trained us to not wait for anything, and while that plays to our advantage 99% of the time, it also eradicates our appreciation and patience for other areas of life which require processes.

Let me assure you that the word "process" is NOT a foul, seven-lettered word—especially in the context of living the life of grace. It is a major part of your journey. Look how Genesis chapter four begins:

> *"Now Adam knew Eve his wife, and she conceived and bore Cain . . . Then she bore again, this time his brother Abel. Now Abel was a keeper of sheep, but Cain was a tiller of the ground. And in the process*

of time it came to pass that Cain brought an offering of the fruit of the ground to the Lord."

Genesis 4:1-3

Notice this phrase, "in the process of time." God has always and will always work in the processes of time. Creation itself was a process (Genesis chapter 1); childbirth is a process, and the Bible says there is a time to plant and a time to harvest. (Ecclesiastes 3:2) Even the birth of Jesus on this earth only occurred "when the fullness of time had come." (Galatians 4:4) Now, if God the Father, knowing there was only one rescue for Mankind, waited for due process to send Jesus, how much more do you think He's orchestrating your due season and process? For some strange reason, we still want everything God has right here and right now!

Consider the life of Paul. Most Christians know his story of conversion, salvation, and call to the ministry, but most do not understand the process he endured to enter that call. In Galatians chapter one, Paul clearly explains how his journey from salvation to ministry took him 21 years! That's right. Not 21 days, weeks, or even months—21 years of preparation and process. Now, I'm not saying that's God's plan for you (Lord, give you patience!), but the principle is true: The journey of the life of grace doesn't happen overnight.

> *The journey of the life of grace doesn't happen overnight.*

Even though it might be hard to swallow sometimes, learning to recognize and live in the process of life carries some tremendous, long-term benefits. Here are a few:

1. **Process develops character.** Usually the people who cringe at going through any type of progression also despise the words "development" and "character." And at the end of the day, those who shortcut the process wind up with very low development and practically no character. No matter how spiritual you may be, no matter how many devils you have cast out of others, let me bring some reality to you: You cannot cast out a lack of development! Neither can you fast and pray enough to persuade God to jump out of time and promote you to places you are not qualified to occupy. It's usually only a disaster waiting to happen.

> *You cannot cast out a lack of development!*

What you can do is embrace and grow through God's plan of development for your life. You're not in it alone; God's grace is there to keep you motivated and grounded. But one word of caution—while grace is leading you through a development stage, don't get frustrated and regress back to the Law. Stay the course, and according to Galatians 6:9, you will reap your harvest in due season IF you do not grow weary and lose heart. Believe me. It pays to embrace the process!

2. **Process removes mess.** Oh, how true this is. Nothing can remove the junk from your life (that will only hinder you later in life) more than the process of time. Even while you might be confessing, "I'm not going to go through stuff in Jesus' name," guess what? You're still going to go through stuff! I've seen people who got saved and God began to develop their life, but

everything on the outside looked like they were going completely backwards! But the truth is sometimes you must go backwards to move forward. Don't be discouraged. It's part of the process, and there is grace to walk it out.

3. **Process means press.** Many times, I have lived in a spot where it felt like God was pressing everything right out of me. Even though I live grace, preach grace, and have heralded this message of grace around the world, there have been times where it seemed like grace was nowhere to be found! I was pressed on every side, and at the time, I couldn't understand all God was up to. It was all part of the process.

    God is pressing you because there is another place He is taking you.

    Let me encourage you that anytime you feel God is pressing you, understand what is truly happening: God is pressing you because there is another place He is taking you. I learned how to *endure the press*, and so will you! During these times, don't make a wrong decision that could stay with you for a lifetime. Don't run away and hide or give up. God's amazing grace is at work—even in the press—even when it doesn't seem like it!

OBEDIENCE IS THE KEY TO BLESSING

While most people know the story of Cain and Abel, they never really understand the whole picture. It's really not a story about jealousy and murder as much as it is about obedience. Genesis 4:4-5 give us the details:

> *"Abel also brought of the firstborn of his flock and of their fat. And the Lord respected Abel and his offering, but He did not respect Cain and his offering."*

Understand that God didn't respect one son over the other, but He did respect one's offering because of obedience. Without going into a lot of detail, Abel's offering was acceptable to God because it was a first-born or first-fruit offering. Abel brought God his first and best, while Cain just brought the Lord "an offering of fruit." God didn't have an issue with the fruit, but it was the priority Cain placed on his offering. Abel sacrificed, was obedient, and brought his best; Cain brought what was leftover. Again, the issue is not what they brought but their obedience.

Let's bring this into where you live today in your journey of faith and grace. Do you realize that you have a specific, holy calling from God which no one else can complete like you? It's true. Everyone does. Where many people seem to miss God is in their act of obedience—completely surrendering to what God has asked them to do. Instead of honoring God with their best, many Christians live frustrated lives by always trying to outsmart God;

or worse yet, complain about how someone else is "living the life they wanted for themselves." But complaining and always trying to play "God" will never bring the blessings that simple obedience will bring.

Obedience, especially when it comes to saying, "Yes God, I will do what You have called me to do" is not always easy. This is especially true during the time of process, character development, and the press. It's so easy to look around at others who are seemingly just going great guns for God and wonder, "What happened to me?" If you are in this type of situation, or if you find yourself analyzing more than obeying, let me give a great scripture to encourage your journey. Take a look:

> **"Having then gifts differing according to the grace that is given to us, let us use them . . . "**
>
> **Romans 12:6**

Notice what the Apostle Paul says here—that we all have gifts, but they are all *different*. Also take note that he did not say they were "competing gifts." Many times, we want to give into our flesh, and instead of obeying God, we would rather compete with others to gain some type of one-up spiritual prize. That's nothing but spiritual immaturity at work. To obey—not to compete—is the key to a life of grace.

There's something else Paul mentions here that is a resounding

...there is no safer place on earth than being in a covenant of obedience before God.

theme of this chapter: "according to the grace that is given to us." This is the second dimension of grace in action. You have a gift from God uniquely designed just for you. You have His grace to do all He has gifted you to do. All of the wisdom, favor, and anointing you will ever need to completely finish your Heavenly assignment is already inside of you. God is for you, not against you, and has equipped you to do your part for the advancement of His Kingdom on the earth. Now, the question is, "Will you be obedient? Will you, like Abel, give God your first and your best or resign to Cain's effort of bringing what's leftover?"

I have witnessed numerous times in my own life and in the lives of others the overwhelming blessings a life of obedience can bring. God is still standing up for those who obey and wholeheartedly walk in their calling. When you do, God's got your back, front, and sides! Believe me, there is no safer place on earth than being in a covenant of obedience before God. Determine in your heart today that you are going to bring your best and walk in obedience to God's plans for your life. This truly is the key to living the life of blessing . . .

. . . The abundant life of God's empowering grace!

DON'T BE A HATER

If you don't quite understand what this section's title means, allow me to explain. In living your journey of grace, and even while fully obeying God with your life, there will always be times where others seem to be blessed with what you thought you deserved! It's inevitable, and the devil will always make sure those people are right up in your view. When this occurs, the issue is what will you do and how will you react? To move into all God has for you, the answer is simple—don't be a hater . . . like Cain!

> *"Now Cain talked with Abel his brother; and it came to pass, when they were in the field, that Cain rose up against Abel his brother and killed him. Then the Lord said to Cain, 'Where is Abel your brother?' He said, 'I do not know. Am I my brother's keeper?'"*

Genesis 4:8-9

Not many people ever stop to think that Cain had an option here. What he should have done was to repent for his disobedience, made an adjustment, and aligned himself to come into the same blessing and favor God granted his younger brother. But he chose the exact opposite and made a decision that would haunt him the rest of his life. Soon after, God confronted Cain about his actions; and even then, he never apologized or took responsibility for his actions but only focused on himself.

Funny, this same thing happens even today!

It's amazing to watch people—especially those God has done so much for—constantly get upset when someone else gets blessed. They can never be content and grateful with what God has so graciously blessed them with, and they always hate on those who receive blessings. It never seems to fail that whenever these same people start going through some tough times—like the press of the process—they attack others who supposedly received "their blessing" even more viciously.

Friend, this is not a part of God's grace in action.

Here's a strong spiritual principle you need to remember for the rest of your life: If you are in trouble in an area of life, don't curse your answer. For instance, if you are in financial trouble, don't curse prosperity or tithing. Don't say, "Well, we tried this tithing thing, and it just didn't work." Maybe you need to change your heart and motives when you tithe. As well, when you see someone else prospering, don't just assume they cheated someone out of the money and got blessed by being dishonest. Rejoice with them in their prosperity knowing that if God did it for them, He will do the same for you! Here's another shift for your thinking:

Take control of your attitude or your attitude will one day take control of you!

Understand that prosperity is not all wealth, and material wealth is not all prosperity. Prosperity is not a *condition*; it's a *position*. Prosperity is not stuff; it's living in God's grace to do what God has anointed you to do! Be thankful for what you already have and treat it like it is a gift from God. I've told many young preachers just starting out in the ministry, "If you only have one suit, clean it every week and be thankful for it!" It's all about your attitude of thankfulness.

The same goes for healing. If you are battling sickness in your body, don't curse healing or get mad at those who get healed. Never curse your answer; instead, make it your friend. Whatever you attack will one day attack you back. It's called the law of reciprocity; or as the Bible says, it's the law of sowing and reaping. (Galatians 6:7)

The Bible also says whatever you think and mediate on, you will become. (See Proverbs 23:7 and Joshua 1:8.) The Scriptures give specific instruction as to what should occupy your mind—

things that are true, noble, honest, lovely, pure, and of good report. (Philippians 4:8) If you find yourself more jealous of others than grateful for what God has blessed you with, here's what you need to do: **stop complaining for 30 solid days!** That's right; every time you want to complain or belly-ache about something or someone, take that same amount of time to be grateful and give God praise for what you do have. It can save your life, change your surroundings, and put you back into the joy of life . . .

. . . On your journey of grace!

NEVER GIVE UP

Much like many other stories in the Old Testament, this one does not end with jealousy and death. Actually, God's incredible grace was already on display even before the Law came into being. Even while Cain's actions resulted in him being "cursed from the earth" (Genesis 4:11) and lived the life of a "fugitive and vagabond on the earth," (Genesis 4:12) God still had another plan at work. You see, while Cain was running, he had a mother, Eve, who was still pressing!

Eve had lost something so precious and valuable to her. Not just one son through death, but now both of the sons God granted her were dislodged from her life. So, what did Eve do? Well, one thing we know she *didn't do*—give up! And her persistence and pursuit paid off. How? Let's take a look at how God's grace was at work even in the midst of a total loss:

...while Cain was running, Eve, was still pressing!

"And Adam knew his wife again, and she bore a son and named him Seth, 'For God has appointed another seed for me instead of Abel, whom Cain killed.'"

Genesis 4:25

What did God do? He displayed his grace by bringing Eve another son! In the midst of what seemed to be a total loss, God brought Eve, Seth. According to the *Vines Expository Dictionary of Old Testament Words*, the name Seth means, "appointed" or "placed." In the midst of a complete tragedy, Eve kept pressing and God birthed another appointed place for her and Adam! And, friend, God is still birthing "Seths" today.

You see, it doesn't matter what you have lost in life that is precious and valuable to you. Maybe it was a great job, a golden opportunity, a divine breakthrough, or a ministry. Maybe you have lost your vision, purpose, direction, or peace of mind. Has God granted you a second, third, or fourth start in life, and you have squandered all of those gracious new beginnings? The possibilities are endless, but no matter what you lost dear to you, there is still great news for you:

GOD HAS SENT YOU A SETH! GOD HAS GIVEN YOU ANOTHER CHANCE! THIS IS YOUR APPOINTED TIME AND PLACE!

This is one of the most powerful elements of the second dimension of grace in action! If you are, or possibly one day will be, in the position where precious things seem to be lost and opportunities wasted, I can truthfully say there is still so much more for you, and it's found in God's empowering grace. Through His grace, you can love again. You can trust again. You can preach, believe, give, befriend, or be faithful in a relationship again.

All because of God's unending grace!

The story doesn't end with Seth, as the Bible says that he had a son named Enosh. The word Enosh literally means "frailty and weakness," but look at what happened from someone who was frail and weak.

> *"And as for Seth, to him also a son was born; and he named him Enosh. Then men began to call on the name of the Lord."*

> **Genesis 4:26**

Adam walked with God in the Garden, but for the first time in the Bible, men began to call on the name of the Lord. Have you noticed that people seldom cry out to God unless they are facing a failure or disaster in life? This is exactly what was happening here as well. The beauty of how this story ends is Seth—Eve's second chance from God's grace—not only brought fulfillment for his mother but also released something out of him which drew men to a closer awareness of God.

Friend, God has given you a Seth. Seize your Seth—your second chance—and an Enosh will be born to you! Don't be afraid to confront your weakness with your frailty. Keep moving forward in your journey of God's second dimension of grace. Don't stop at the destination of salvation but keep perpetuating the grace of God to others around you and to future generations to come. All the time, while you are enduring processes, walking in obedience, and rejoicing with those who are blessed around you, always remember to never, ever give up on God's grace! Oh, and don't forget . . .

. . . To enjoy the journey!

CHAPTER 11

STAY WITH GRACE

I t is my prayer that over the course of this book God has revealed something about His grace or solidified the purpose, power, and working of His grace for your life. His grace is sufficient and reaches farther than any human mind could ever comprehend. Aren't you glad God's saving grace led you to salvation? And aren't you glad His empowering grace has provided everything you need to accomplish all of His will and plans for you in this life?

His grace is amazing and extravagant!

As you journey with God, let me be the first to encourage you to learn all you can about the grace which is so easily available to you. Don't ever settle for anything less than His grace in action. Don't let anyone ever convince you that you've gone too far or have blown it too many times for God's grace to be rendered ineffective in your life. That's a lie straight from hell. Keep walking in grace!

I believe the greatest teacher of grace, outside of Jesus, was the Apostle Paul. Many times throughout this book, we have seen his writings and revelation of grace which is still changing and shaping our view of God today. Apparently, Paul was faced with some of the same religious mindsets as we have today. Funny how some things just never change! That mindset was prevalent in the Church at Galatia which led to Paul writing a strong charge to the church concerning their continuing in the truth that they had heard. Look at what he wrote:

> *"O foolish Galatians! Who has bewitched you that you should not obey the truth . . . Did you receive the Spirit by the works of the law, or by the hearing of faith? Are you so foolish? Having begun in the Spirit, are you now being made perfect by the flesh?"*

Galatians 3:1-3

Notice the word "bewitched." It implies the working of witchcraft. In other words, Paul addresses those who started their walk in grace and then reverted back to legalism as, "Who put a spell on you? Who contaminated your thinking with old, dead, religious ideology and thoughts?" He continues by asking, "Why did you start out in the Spirit, but then resorted back to ways of the Law? If you started in grace, why not finish in grace?" Honestly, I think he would be asking these same questions to the Church at large today.

Friend, let me encourage you to not be like the foolish Galatian Church and go backwards from where you are today. God poured everything He had out for you, and only His grace makes His abundant life accessible. Now that you have seen this wonderful gift and how it can eternally impact your life—not only in Heaven but here on this earth as well—don't go back to the Law. Stay free from what religious mindsets will tell you. Walk free from condemnation and the guilt of sin. Live under the fountain of grace which is freely poured out upon you! I promise you will never regret turning away from the Law and living under God's unending grace.

Let me also encourage you to never settle for anything less than God's best for your life. Remember, the second dimension of grace is the equipping for you to live out God's purpose on this earth. Don't spend your time chasing after somebody else's anointing or gifting. Why would you want something that is second best? The truth is you are as anointed as you are ever going to be . . . *right now!* You can never bargain God into giving you somebody else's grace by fasting or praying. It just won't happen. Change your pursuit from chasing those who dangle the proverbial "anointing carrot" in front of your eyes to chasing after more revelation of God's empowering grace.

That is where you will find your equipping and anointing!

God's empowering grace is the element which enables you to live holy and to walk in all the anointing you need to accomplish your mission on this planet. God's grace is what reveals and provides you with every gift you will need to fulfill your purpose and destiny. It's His amazing grace which supernaturally equips and qualifies you to live the abundant life Jesus promised. Whether your desire is to be anointed, blessed, favored—whatever the case may be—all of these are found and released in one remarkable place:

God's unending grace!

Shift your thinking from what God is going to do to what He has already done. Realign your thoughts from what God saved you from to living and walking in His empowering grace. You will be truly amazed how your life will radically change when your thoughts and intents shift from the Law to God's supernatural grace. Remember, you are redeemed from the curse of the Law, and nobody can curse you. So, I challenge you to change your confession from "I'm redeemed from the curse" to "Since I am redeemed from the curse of Law, here is how a redeemed person acts, thinks, and lives!" Do you see the difference? It's a shift of thinking.

In each of Paul's 13 letters in the New Testament, his saluta-tions all contained the same greeting: "Grace to you and peace from our Father and the Lord Jesus Christ." Apparently, Paul knew the importance of emphasizing the power of grace and peace. I believe these two words, much like "truth and grace," compliment and are attached to each other for a reason. And that reason is simply:

To truly live a life of peace, you must walk in the grace of God!

Friend, as you go forward in this wonderful adventure of grace, let peace be your guide; meaning, whenever you feel your life is not surrounded and led by peace, step back a minute and check your grace walk! Look around to see if you are living under the fountain of grace or have you slipped back into a life ruled by the Law? Also, check your grace walk with others. Are you a living example of God's grace in action—full of truth and grace—or have you resorted back to a condemning attitude towards those you know and love? Finally, check the level of grace you are extending to yourself. Living under the weight of self-condemnation will automatically render God's peace ineffective in your life. Can you see what common element is necessary to live the abundant life of peace God has so freely given you? The grace of God!

In every aspect of life, go with God, go with peace, and most importantly, make the shift to go with grace!

You will be eternally glad you did.

ABOUT THE AUTHOR

Archbishop David Huskins has often been called a dreamer mainly due to the tremendous vision and calling from God which rest upon his life. Bishop Huskins is a true apostle who carries a prophetic mantle. He serves as the presiding bishop of the International Communion of Charismatic Churches (ICCC), an international organization representing over 4.2 million people. He also is the founder and senior pastor of Cedar Lake Christian Center (CLCC) in Cedartown, Georgia which is a working prototype of a true Vineyard Harvest church. Bishop Huskins believes that reaching the outcast and unwanted should be the "norm" and not the exception; thus, CLCC has focused on ministry to HIV/Aids patients, jails and prisons, and a highly acclaimed ministry to the chemically addicted.

In 1990, Bishop Huskins was presented an honorary doctorate of education degree by Universal Faith Kingdom Academy. He finished his doctorate of theology in Biblical studies from Florida Theological Seminary in 1998, was bestowed a doctorate of divinity degree in 2004 by Saint Thomas Christian College, and serves as the chancellor of Vineyard Harvester Bible College.

Bishop Huskins hosts a weekly radio program, *A Call to Covenant*, and is a frequent guest host for many television programs on the TCT Network and Daystar. He has also appeared as a guest on TBN. He is the author of *The Power of the Covenant Heart* and *The Purpose of the Covenant Heart*, both released by Destiny Image Publishers. He has four sons: Aaron, Zachary, Isaac, and Michael.

Above all, Bishop Huskins is a servant of God!

CONTACT INFORMATION

Archbishop David Huskins
International Communion of Charismatic Churches
P. O. Box 687
Cedartown, GA 30125
770-748-5750
www.theiccc.com
www.clccnet.org

For more books, DVDs, and other resources
by David Huskins
Visit our online store at:
www.clccnet.org